Your Guinea Pig

A Kid's Guide to Raising and Showing

WANDA L. CURRAN

A Garden Way Publishing Book

Storey Communications, Inc.
Schoolhouse Road
Pownal, Vermont 05261

Acknowledgments

Thank-you to John, Bertie, Lexi, Terril, Jim, and Louise, all of whom endured the writing of this book by proofreading before the manuscript went to the editor. A special thank-you to Monique and her crew for the close-up photos my camera could not manage.

Edited by Lorin A. Driggs and Deborah Balmuth
Cover and text design by Carol J. Jessop
Cover photograph © Positive Images/Patricia J. Bruno
Text production by Wanda Harper Joyce
Photographs by Wanda L. Curran unless noted otherwise
Line drawings by Jeffrey C. Domm
Technical review by Sheri Schlorman, D.V.M.
Indexed by Northwind Editorial Services

The information in this book is true and complete to the best of our knowledge. All recommendations are made without guarantee on the part of the author or Storey Communications, Inc. The author and publisher disclaim any liability in connection with the use of this information. For additional information, please contact Storey Communications, Inc., Schoolhouse Road, Pownal, Vermont 05261.

Garden Way Publishing was founded in 1973 as part of the Garden Way Incorporated Group of Companies, dedicated to bringing gardening information and equipment to as many people as possible. Today the name "Garden Way Publishing" is licensed to Storey Communications, Inc., in Pownal, Vermont. For a complete list of Garden Way Publishing titles call 1-800-827-8673. Garden Way Incorporated manufactures products in Troy, New York, under the Troy-Bilt® brand including garden tillers, chipper/shredders, mulching mowers, sicklebar mowers, and tractors. For information on any Garden Way Incorporated product, please call 1-800-345-4454.

Printed in the United States by Capital City Press
First Printing, April 1995

Library of Congress Cataloging-in-Publication Data

Curran, Wanda, 1949-
    Your guinea pig : a kid's guide to raising and showing / Wanda L. Curran.
        p.   cm.
    "A Garden Way Publishing book."
    Includes bibliographical references (p.   ) and index.
    ISBN 0-88266-889-7 (pb) : $12.95
      1. Guinea pigs as pets—Juvenile literature. [1. Guinea pigs. 2. Pets.] I. Title.
SF459.G9C94 1995
636'.93234—dc20
                                        94-42164
                                           CIP
                                         AC

Dedication

This book is dedicated to
my 4-H cavy project members, past, present, and future,
without whom it would not have been written.

Contents

A Few Words to Parents

Children always want a pet. "I'll feed him. I'll clean his cage," promises an eager would-be pet owner. The problem is that young children may not comprehend the real responsibility of pet ownership. It helps when responsibility for a pet is really a partnership between parents and young children. A guinea pig is a very easy way to begin introducing responsibility for the care of pets to your child.

Guinea pigs are becoming more and more popular as pets because they require little space, are nearly odorless, and can even be raised in an apartment in the city. The fact that they are relatively inexpensive to purchase and house is also a factor in the growing popularity of guinea pigs as pets and hobbies.

Raising a guinea pig can be a very rewarding and educational experience for both you and your child. Being there to support and help your child learn the fun and the work of raising this extraordinary little creature is one of the best ways to teach responsibility. You may be amazed at how many things you and your child can find to talk about as you hold the guinea pig while he or she cleans the cage.

There is almost no limit to the knowledge your child can gain by raising guinea pigs, including valuable lessons about life, death, birth, organization of chores, and planning for the future. As your child matures, she or he may learn business sense and something about ethics when dealing with customers. Your child also may discover many new interests and new talents because of the knowledge gained from this wonderful hobby.

One last thought. Ninety-nine percent of the time, the choice of your child's first guinea pig will be a matter of heart rather than knowledge. Once the first guinea pig has been chosen, the real fun and learning about guinea pigs begin. Even though this first pet may not be perfect for showing, it will likely be treasured for as long as it lives.

Here is an idea that may help you help your child make the best possible choice for a first guinea pig. If it is possible, go in advance and find several suitable guinea pigs. Then allow your child to choose, among these select few, that very special pet of the heart.

The adventure begins. Learn and work together, but above all else, have patience and have fun.

Introduction

Because of their size, guinea pigs make wonderful pets even for children as young as 5 years old. Adult guinea pigs weigh 2 to 4 pounds, which makes them easier to handle than larger pets. Guinea pigs also have very good temperaments. They are not as likely to bite as hamsters, rats, mice, gerbils, and other *rodents* kept as pets; they do not have the annoying, strong, musky odors for which other rodents are known. They are not particularly inclined to climb, jump, or chew, which makes housing guinea pigs easier than housing other rodents. The personality of guinea pigs is A+.

Guinea pig is the common name for the *cavy.* Cavy is short for the species name *Cavia porcellus.* Under the family name of Caviidae, guinea pigs are described as South American rodents with no visible tail, a single pair of *mammae,* four toes on each forefoot, and three toes on each hind foot.

It is funny that this delightful little animal, which neither comes from Guinea nor is a pig, is called a guinea pig. The most accepted explanation for the name is that the animals do grunt and squeal something like a pig and were sold by British sailors for a guinea, an old English coin.

If guinea pigs are given good care they may live 5 to 7 years. They are strictly *herbivorous,* which means

The personality of guinea pigs is A+.

Herbivorous. *Plant-eating.*

Recognized Guinea Pig Breeds

- Abyssinian
- Abyssinian Satin
- American
- American Satin
- Peruvian
- Peruvian Satin
- Silkie
- Silkie Satin
- Teddy
- Teddy Satin
- White Crested

plant-eating. They have a continuous breeding season, though they do not breed as often as other rodents. Guinea pigs usually have small *litters* of 1 to 3 pups. Guinea pigs can see and hear, have a full coat of hair, have teeth, and are able to walk and nibble at food within hours after birth.

At the present time, there are eleven recognized *breeds* of guinea pigs. Each breed includes a number of colors and color patterns called *varieties*. There are twenty-three recognized varieties shown in each breed except the White Crested. Only seventeen White Crested varieties are shown.

Choosing Your Guinea Pig

W hether you are looking only for a pet or are planning to show your guinea pig, the cost of care is the same. You should always try to make the best choice possible.

Breed. A class of guinea pigs that reproduces young with its distinctive characteristics.

Which Breed?

Probably the most important thing you need to decide is how much time you have for grooming or how much time you wish to spend on grooming. This will help determine which breed of guinea pig you should choose. A breed is a class of guinea pigs that reproduces young with its distinctive characteristics of markings, texture, type, size, and coat pattern.

American

The American guinea pig is the most common breed available and it is also the easiest to groom. The coat of the American guinea pig is short and smooth, lying close to the skin. Grooming is as simple as rubbing the hair from head to rump with your hand.

American

DEBBIE MCKEACHNIE

Abyssinian

Abyssinian

The Abyssinian guinea pig is not as common as the American. The coat of the Abyssinian is short but wiry and has a distinct growth pattern. The Abyssinian's hair grows in whorls and ridges that stick out from the body. The whorls are called *rosettes*. On a good, showable Abyssinian, there must be two shoulder rosettes, four saddle rosettes, two hip rosettes, and two rump rosettes. All of this makes for some special grooming procedures that can take a little time.

Peruvian

Peruvian

Peruvian guinea pigs have long, smooth coats. The hair grows from the shoulders over the sides and rump and over the head and face. The hair parts down the middle of the back. If you can't tell the front from the back, you're probably looking at a good Peruvian. The Peruvian's long hair takes a great deal of time to care for even when the guinea pig is young. A Peruvian must have its hair wrapped often and even be bathed and blow-dried. (See "Grooming Your Guinea Pig," page 76.)

Silkie

Silkie

The Silkie guinea pig also has a long, smooth coat, but the head and face are not covered by the long hair, and there is no part down the middle of the back. The Silkie also needs to have its hair wrapped often and to be bathed and blow-dried. (See "Grooming Your Guinea Pig," page 76.) Grooming a Silkie guinea pig can require a lot of time.

Teddy

The Teddy is a very popular breed of guinea pig. A Teddy has a short, wiry, kinky coat that sticks out from the body. The coat has a very plush feeling much like a good stuffed teddy bear. Routine grooming of this breed is as simple as rubbing the hair backward from rump to head, but deep cleaning with combs and brushes takes more time.

Teddy

White Crested

The White Crested guinea pig has a short, smooth coat like the American, with a single white rosette on the forehead. Grooming a White Crested is much like grooming the American — rubbing the hair from shoulder to rump with your hand. A little extra care is needed for the single rosette.

White Crested

Other Breeds

There are American Satin, Abyssinian Satin, Peruvian Satin, Silkie Satin, and Teddy Satin guinea pigs. Satins are just like the above-mentioned breeds except that they have a hollow hair shaft that gives the hair a wonderful sheen. Grooming Satins is the same as grooming the other breeds described above.

Crossbreeds

Crossbreed guinea pigs may have long hair, short hair, or an unusual combination of hair growth. Crossbreeds are guinea pigs whose parents are of different breeds. Crossbreeds do not reproduce young with their distinct characteristics of markings, texture, type, size, coat pattern, etc. While crossbreeds can't win ribbons at shows for purebred guinea pigs, they still must be groomed. Long hair takes a lot of grooming time to stay looking its best, and short hair takes a minimum of grooming time.

Peruvian X Abyssinian crossbreed. This pig is not eligible for showing, but makes a very cute pet.

Which Variety?

Variety. A subdivision of a breed based on color.

Another choice you will need to make is the variety of guinea pig you would like to own. A variety is a subdivision of a breed based on color of hair and/or color of eyes and color pattern. Varieties are organized into groups based on how the color is distributed on the hair shaft and over the whole body of a guinea pig. There are 23 recognized guinea pig varieties. The following is a brief description of most of the accepted varieties of guinea pigs in the groups to which they belong. The *Standard of Perfection* will give a more thorough and complete description. (See "Choosing a Show-Quality Guinea Pig," page 11.) Your choice of variety should be based on what you like. It will also be based on which varieties are available for you to choose from and their quality.

Self Group

The *Self* group is composed of varieties in which the hair shaft is all one color from tip to base (where the hair grows out of the skin), and the guinea pig is only one color from nose to rump.

Beige is light brown, with matching ears and footpads, and pink eyes.

Black is deep, rich black with black eyes.

Chocolate is the color of bittersweet chocolate (not light milk chocolate or dark unsweetened bakers' chocolate). A chocolate should have dark eyes with a ruby cast or brown eyes.

Lilac is light gray with a purple cast. The pink or dark eyes may or may not have a ruby cast.

Red-eyed Orange is reddish orange (ears and footpads must match) with ruby red eyes.

Red is the color of an Irish setter dog. The ears and footpads should be dark in color but not black, and the eyes should be dark.

White is China white with pink or dark eyes with or without a ruby cast.

Agouti Group

The *Agouti* group is made up of varieties that have a hair shaft with two different colors (a tip color and a darker base color) and *ticking*. Ticking is the longer hairs (called guard hairs) dispersed throughout the coat. They are the same color as the base color of the rest of the coat but have a black tip. These combinations of colored hairs are evenly intermingled over the body of the guinea pig except for the belly. The belly of an agouti has no ticking. Instead, a narrow band of hair from the chin to the genital area matches the tip color.

The golden agouti variety has hair with a red tip and a black base, the ticking is black, and the bellyband is red with no ticking.

The silver agouti has hair with a white tip and a black base, the ticking is black, and the bellyband is white with no ticking.

The dilute agouti variety is made up of any combination of these tip and base colors:

Tip Color	Base Color
Cream	Beige
Orange	Black
Red	Chocolate
White	Lilac

Remember that on an agouti, the ticking color must match the base color and the bellyband color must match the tip color and have no ticking.

Solid Group

The *Solid* group is composed of varieties in which there is more than one color of hair and/or the hair shaft is more than one color. The colors blend together to make a distinct appearance and the guinea pig is this combination of color from nose to rump.

Ticking. Longer hairs, called guard hairs, dispersed throughout a guinea pig's coat.

Roan. *The even distri-bution of white hair with any other colored hair.*

Roan is the even distribution of white hair with any other colored hair. For example, a black roan has black hair and white hair. Black and white are intermingled, giving the appearance of salt and pepper mixed together thoroughly. Red or strawberry roan is red hair intermingled with white hair. The hair color is intermingled over the whole body of the guinea pig. A roan guinea pig may or may not have the intermingling of color on the head. For showing purposes, 75 percent or more of the body must have the intermingling of color.

Brindle. *The intermin-gling of red and black hair.*

Brindle is the intermingling of red and black hair, every other hair to be black and red. The effect is the same as roan but only the red and black combination is allowed. To be shown, the body of a brindle must have the intermingling of the red and black over 60 percent of the body.

Dilute solid is the same as dilute agouti without a bellyband, and the color combinations are over the entire body.

Golden solid is the same as golden agouti without a bellyband.

Silver solid is the same as the silver agouti without a bellyband.

Marked Group

The *Marked* group is made up of varieties with specific patterns of colored patches.

Broken. *Two or more distinct patches of color distributed over the body and head.*

Broken guinea pigs have two or more colors distributed in patches over the body and head. A broken may be white and red, black and white, golden agouti, red and white, and so on. Each patch of color must be distinct from any other patch of color. Each color must have at least one patch the size of a 50-cent piece or larger. Other patches may be smaller or larger.

A *Dalmatian* guinea pig is white with spots. The spots may be any color in the self group and the eyes should go with the color of the spots.

A *Dutch* guinea pig must have a white collar, chest,

forelegs, blaze, and *foot stops*. The rest of the guinea pig may be any other self or agouti color.

A *Himalayan* guinea pig must be white with a black nose, black ears, black feet, and pink eyes.

A *tortoise shell* (sometimes called TS) guinea pig may only have color patches of red and black with dark eyes. Each color must cover a minimum of ¼ of the guinea pig.

Tortoise shell and white (sometimes called TSW) is red, black, and white. The guinea pig should be divided in half down the center of the back and the color patches alternated from side to side. Each color must have at least one patch the size of a 50-cent piece (a little bigger than a quarter) or larger. The eyes of a TSW should be dark.

Which Sex?

After you have picked a breed and a variety, your next decision is what sex your guinea pig will be — a male, called a *boar,* or a female, called a *sow.* That decision should be based on the reason you want this guinea pig. Will this be a single pet? Will this be a single show guinea pig? Do you want to breed your guinea pig?

It really does not matter which sex you choose if your guinea pig will be a single pet or a single show animal. If you are interested in breeding guinea pigs, the sex of your first guinea pig can make a difference.

If you want to begin with only one guinea pig and then breed at a later time, you should begin with a boar. That's because a sow must be bred (mated to produce young) and should give birth before she is one year of age. It may not be possible to find a suitable boar to breed to your sow in the limited time during which she must be bred. With a boar, you can take as much time as you need to find a sow to breed him to. Another reason for starting with a boar is that a boar may be shown even when he is in breeding.

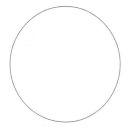

This circle is the size of a 50-cent piece.

Boar. *A male guinea pig.*

Sow. *A female guinea pig.*

A sow should not be shown while she is pregnant or before she has recovered from caring for her litter.

Which Breeder?

Before you get down to the nitty-gritty of choosing your show-quality guinea pig, take some time to see and talk to as many *breeders* as possible. Breeders are people who breed and raise guinea pigs on a regular basis. Talking to many breeders will help you learn about the characteristics that are desirable in the breed you've chosen. You will also learn who is knowledge-able and what price to expect to pay for your guinea pig. You can find the names of breeders through your local 4–H office, at local pet stores and feed stores, or at local rabbit and cavy shows. You can also get information by writing to the American Rabbit Breeders Association (A.R.B.A.) or the American Cavy Breeders Association (A.C.B.A.). (You'll find the addresses in *Helpful Sources* at the back of this book.)

See the breeder's *caviary* if at all possible. A caviary is the place where guinea pigs are raised. Seeing where a guinea pig was raised and the type of care it received will give you a better idea about its general health before you purchase it.

Above all, make sure you feel comfortable with the breeder before you buy a guinea pig. If for some reason you do not feel comfortable dealing with a particular breeder, find a different one.

Which Guinea Pig?

Now is the time to make that most important decision: which guinea pig to choose. Whether you are getting a pet or a show animal, be sure to see as many guinea pigs as possible so you can make the best choice.

Choosing a Pet

Choosing a pet-quality guinea pig or a pet-quality breeding guinea pig is as easy as finding one that has a good personality as well as eye appeal.

Choosing a Show-Quality Guinea Pig

Choosing a show-quality guinea pig or a show-quality breeding guinea pig is a little more complicated. To begin, study the *Standard of Perfection* from the American Rabbit Breeders Association, Inc. This book tells you just what the guinea pig you want should look like. It explains what characteristics are not acceptable in show-quality guinea pigs of the breed or variety you are considering. In particular, the *Standard* will help you identify *faults* and *disqualifications*. A fault is a characteristic that keeps a guinea pig's appearance from being perfect for its type (breed and variety). A disqualification makes a guinea pig unshowable.

Another helpful strategy is to ask the breeder to show you a better animal than the one you are considering and a worse one, and to explain the differences.

Choosing a Healthy Guinea Pig

You naturally want to choose the healthiest guinea pig possible. Take a few minutes to study the parts of the guinea pig. This will help you know where to look when you examine a guinea pig you are interested in owning. The following is a simple step-by-step guide to help you choose a healthy guinea pig.

Examine the eyes. The eyes should be bold and clear, with no signs of film over them or discharge. Check for *pea eye* (see "Keeping Your Guinea Pig Healthy," page 47). In a show animal, the eyes must be the correct color for the breed and variety.

Examine the ears. The ears should be clean on the inside, with no wax buildup and no dirty, reddish–brown waxlike matter, which is a symptom of ear mites. Check for *lice* and *mites* around the ears. If this guinea pig is for show, are the ears the correct color,

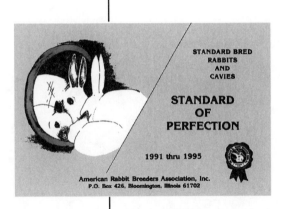

This book has pictures and descriptions of every guinea pig breed.

Fault. *A characteristic that keeps a guinea pig's appearance from being perfect for its type.*

Disqualification. *A defect that makes a guinea pig unshowable.*

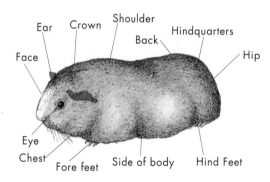

The parts of a Guinea Pig

Ear | Crown | Shoulder | Back | Hindquarters | Hip | Face | Eye | Chest | Fore feet | Side of body | Hind Feet

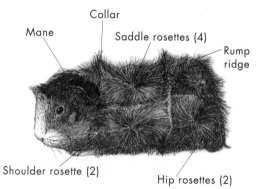

The parts of the Abyssinian

Mane | Collar | Saddle rosettes (4) | Rump ridge | Shoulder rosette (2) | Hip rosettes (2)

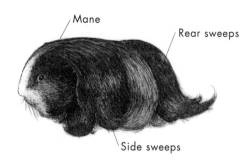

The parts of the Silkie

Mane | Rear sweeps | Side sweeps

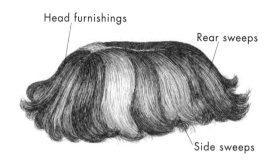

The parts of the Peruvian

Head furnishings | Rear sweeps | Side sweeps

with hair and flesh matching? Are the ears properly positioned? Are there any undesirable rips?

Examine the nose. The nose should be free of any signs of discharge. For a show animal, is the nose properly shaped (flat and broad, narrow and pointy, Roman) for this breed, as described in the *Standard of Perfection?*

Examine the teeth and mouth. The mouth should be clean. The teeth should be straight, without chips. When the mouth is closed, the top front teeth should be just in front of and overlapping the bottom front teeth. There should be no sign of slobbering or drooling.

Examine the chin and neck. You should feel no lumps or bumps around the chin or neck.

Examine the legs. All four legs should be straight when you gently feel along the bone. Examine the hair on the inside of the front legs near the feet to see if there is any sign of matted hair. Matted hair on the inside of the front legs tells you that the guinea pig has been cleaning a runny nose and should not be considered for purchase.

Examine the feet and toes. There should be four toes and toenails on each front foot and three toes and toenails on each rear foot. The nails should be trimmed neatly. The footpads on the bottom of the feet should not have any sores or tender spots. Are the toenails the correct color for this variety? (This matters only if you will be showing your new guinea pig or using it to breed show animals.)

Examine the genitals. Is this a boar or sow? The genital and vent area should be clean, with no signs of diarrhea or other discharge. There should be no pimples, sores, or bad odors.

Examine the chest and abdomen. There should be no lumps, bumps, or *hernias* as you feel along the chest and abdomen.

On a show animal, extra toes or missing toes or toenails are not acceptable. In addition, this trait may be inherited by offspring, so a guinea pig with missing or extra toes should not be used for breeding.

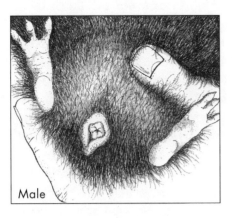

Male

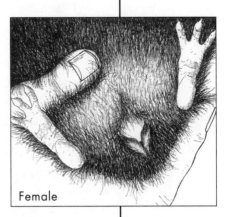

Female

Compare the genital area of your guinea pig with these drawings of the adult boar, left, and the adult sow, right.

Examine the hair and skin. The hair should be clean, shiny, and even all over. There should be no bare patches or areas that look chewed. The hair should not come out when you pet the guinea pig. The skin should look healthy, with no dandruff or scaliness. There should be no sores or scratches. Look closely for lice (tiny bugs) around the rump. On a show animal, look for foreign colored hair — hair that is the wrong color for a particular variety. Check the texture, density, and length of the hair. Check the color and the depth of color. If there are patches of color, look for clean lines of demarcation between the colors. Are the patches of color the correct size for the variety? Check the percentage of roan or brindling (see page 8).

Examine the shoulders. On a show-quality guinea pig, the shoulders should be as wide as the hips.

Watch the guinea pig move. The guinea pig should walk and run smoothly, with a sort of fast shuffle. It should not limp or drag any of its limbs.

Observe the guinea pig's behavior. The guinea pig should be alert and inquisitive.

Observe the guinea pig's appetite. Does the guinea pig eat frequently? If you are with the guinea pig for only a short time, offer a treat. The guinea pig should readily accept it.

Check the guinea pig's breathing. Make sure the guinea pig breathes in a regular rhythm. There should be no noise produced when the guinea pig breathes.

Examine overall appearance. If this guinea pig is for show, does the head balance with the body? Do the ears balance with the head, or do they look too big or too small for this guinea pig? Are the eyes too small?

Ask about breeding history. If you are considering getting an older guinea pig that will be used for breeding, you'll need to find out if it has been bred before. If the guinea pig is a sow, ask when she was last bred. What was the litter size? Were there any special needs or problems during or after the pregnancy?

Checklist for Selecting a Healthy Pet or Show-Quality Guinea Pig

- ☐ Type
- ☐ Disqualifications
- ☐ Ears (clean; set properly; correct color for variety)
- ☐ Eyes (clear, bright, bold; correct color for variety)
- ☐ Nose (clean; no discharge)
- ☐ Mouth, teeth (clean, no drooling; teeth straight, top overlap bottom)
- ☐ Chin, neck (no lumps or bumps)
- ☐ Legs, feet (straight, no matted hair; no extra or missing toes or nails; nails correct color for type; footpads correct color)
- ☐ Chest, abdomen (no lumps or hernias)
- ☐ Genitals (boar, sow; clean, no sores, pimples, or bad odors)
- ☐ Hair, skin (clean, shiny, no dandruff, scratches, scaliness; no lice or mites; correct color for type)
- ☐ Shoulders (wide as hips)
- ☐ Movement (fast shuffle, no limping or dragging of limbs)
- ☐ Appetite (eats frequently, readily accepts treat)
- ☐ Alert, inquisitive
- ☐ Has the guinea pig been bred before?
- ☐ When was the sow last bred?
- ☐ What was the litter size?
- ☐ Were there any special needs or problems during or after the pregnancy?

Pedigree. A document identifying the parents and ancestors of a purebred guinea pig.

Quarantine. To isolate a guinea pig from other guinea pigs to prevent the spread of illness.

Before You Take Your New Guinea Pig Home

Once you've chosen your new guinea pig, you'll need the answers to these questions in order to help it adjust to its new home:

- Which brand of feed is this guinea pig used to? (Ask for a small supply to take home with you.)

- What treats is this guinea pig used to? (Ask for a small supply so your new guinea pig will have treats until you can stock up.)

- Where has the guinea pig normally been housed — indoors or outdoors?

A Pedigree for Your Show Guinea Pig

If you plan to show your guinea pig or use it for breeding show animals, try to get one with a *pedigree*. A pedigree is a document provided by the seller identifying the *purebred* parents and ancestors of the guinea pig for at least three previous generations. The pedigree will tell you about colors or varieties in the family background of the guinea pig. It will also tell you if your new guinea pig is related, in any way, to any guinea pigs you may already own. (See "Managing Your Caviary," page 124.)

Quarantine

If you already have one or more guinea pigs, it is very important to *quarantine* the new guinea pig for three to four weeks. When you quarantine a guinea pig, you keep it away from the rest of your guinea pigs, preferably in a separate room. Sometimes a guinea pig is in the very beginning stages of an illness but does not show any signs of illness at the time of purchase. If your newly purchased guinea pig should become ill during the quarantine period, none of the rest of your guinea pigs will be exposed to the illness and then become ill also. You can spare yourself a lot of unhappiness and expense by remembering to quarantine all new guinea pigs no matter who sold them to you.

Guinea Pig Housing and Equipment

Guinea pigs should only be housed individually or in colonies with other guinea pigs.

Boars born and raised together may be kept together in a colony. Once a boar is separated from a colony for more than a few hours, he may not be returned to a colony that includes other boars because the boars will fight. Do not try to introduce a new boar into a cage with one or more other boars.

Sows usually do not fight, but when you place a sow in a new colony, watch closely to make sure everyone is getting along. Even guinea pigs that get along sometimes get into scuffles that can cause minor injuries. Guinea pigs also sometimes chew each other's hair. For these reasons, you should house your show animals in separate individual cages.

Guinea pigs should be housed indoors where the temperature can be maintained at 68° to 72° Fahrenheit. To prevent illness, keep the temperature as constant as possible, with no sudden changes. Position cages so the guinea pigs receive 14 to 16 hours of light each day, but not in direct sunlight. The light may need to be artificial. To

Guinea pigs should not be housed with other species, such as rabbits, rats, mice, and hamsters. Not only do they have different nutritional requirements, but other rodents may carry diseases that are fatal to guinea pigs and vice versa.

A good guinea pig cage . . .

- Keeps your guinea pig from getting out.

- Protects your guinea pig from other pets.

- Allows you easy access to your guinea pig.

- Allows easy cleaning.

- Allows enough space for exercise and comfort and does not soil too quickly.

A plastic-and-wire cage is one suitable choice for a guinea pig house.

help prevent colds and heatstroke, make sure cages are away from drafts and direct sunlight.

Cages

You can buy a guinea pig cage at a pet or feed store or you can make one.

The size of a guinea pig cage depends on how many guinea pigs will live there and their condition — whether they are growing, full-grown, or breeding. A single full-grown guinea pig needs a cage that is at least 18 inches by 18 inches by 12 to 15 inches high. A pregnant sow or a sow with a litter should have a cage 24 inches by 24 inches by 12 to 15 inches high or larger depending on the size of the litter. A space of 30 inches by 36 inches by 12 to 15 inches high may house one boar with five sows for breeding.

Aquariums, wire cages, wood-and-wire cages, wood cages, plastic-and-wire cages, or even a child's plastic wading pool all make suitable houses for guinea pigs. If you have other pets, an aquarium or wading pool will need a good screen to serve as a cover or lid. If your guinea pigs will be housed in a slightly cooler area, such as a garage, aquariums or all wood cages will help keep them warm.

Wire or screen used for guinea pig cages should have a grid of not more than 1 inch by 2 inches. Anything larger may allow guinea pigs to escape, especially young ones. A cage may open on the side or top to give you access to your guinea pig. It is most important that the floor be solid rather than wire. A wire floor will cause stress in guinea pigs and may cause broken toenails, toes, feet, or legs.

Be sure to thoroughly check your guinea pig's cage for loose wires, splinters, sharp edges, or anything that may cause injury. Fix any of these problems by cutting, sanding, or covering before you put your guinea pig in the cage. Examine your guinea pig's cage for possible dangers each time you clean it.

Doors should close securely to prevent your guinea pig from escaping or other animals from getting into the cage.

One type of cage that is easy to clean has all wire sides, a wire top, and a metal or plastic tray for a floor. The cage may lift out of the tray or the tray may slide out of the cage. Either way, the tray and cage are light and easy to clean thoroughly. Top-opening cages are particularly good for pregnant sows. You can remove the soiled bedding without dismantling the cage or moving a very pregnant sow who is close to giving birth.

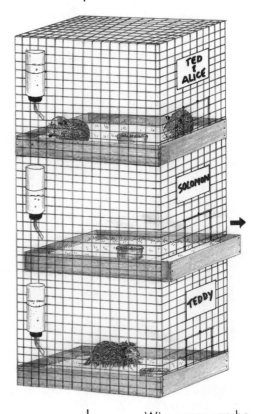

Wire cages can be stacked to house several guinea pigs.

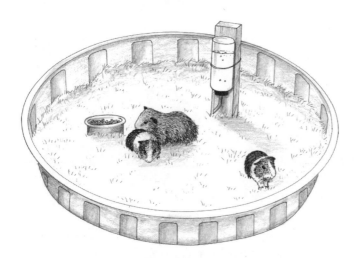

A guinea pig house can be made from a plastic wading pool.

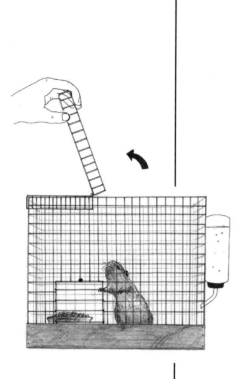

A top-opening cage
makes it easy to reach
your guinea pig.

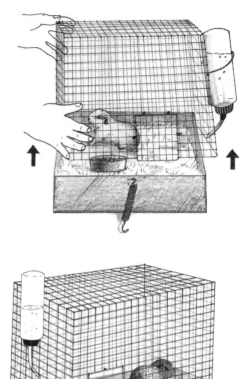

A cage that lifts out of the floor tray (top)
or one with a slide-out tray (bottom)
is easy to clean.

Bedding

Guinea pigs need bedding that absorbs waste and is safe
to eat. (Guinea pigs do on occasion chew and/or eat
bedding materials.) Pine or fir wood shavings, or a
combination of the two, are absorbent and safe for a
guinea pig to chew or eat. Straw is good for warmth,
but it is not as absorbent as shavings. Straw also breaks
long hair and therefore should not be used as bedding

for Peruvians or Silkies. Pellet-type, commercial bedding is also available. Cedar shavings may smell nice, but the oils may be harmful to guinea pigs.

All bedding should be changed before it becomes wet or soggy, usually every 2 to 3 days. All shavings and commercial bedding should be checked for large splinters that can injure your guinea pig's feet.

On occasion, you may not be able to get proper bedding when you need it. In a pinch, use clean, shredded newspaper that is several days old; fresh newsprint can be toxic to guinea pigs.

Feed Storage

Feed needs to be stored in waterproof, airtight containers to keep it as fresh as possible. Air, heat, moisture, and light can damage the nutrients in feed, especially vitamin C.

Food Dish or Feeder

Your guinea pig's food dish must be heavy to prevent it from being tipped over, spilling the feed into dirty bedding. The dish or crock should not be large enough for your guinea pig to sit in and use as a bathroom.

If you use a feeder instead of a dish or crock, place it a little above the floor so that dirty bedding and feces cannot get into the food. A metal J-feeder fits through a hole in the side of a wire cage and is easily filled from the outside. A metal or plastic outside feeder does not take up any space inside the cage and is a good choice for smaller cages.

Food crock

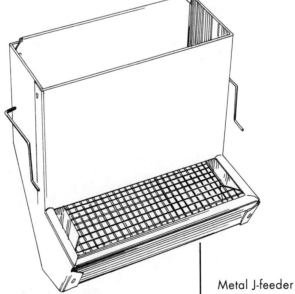

Metal J-feeder

A plastic water bottle with metal sipper tube will help keep your guinea pig's water clean.

Water Bottle

A bowl or crock should not be used for your guinea pig's water because it will allow bacteria to grow that can make a guinea pig very ill. A plastic water bottle with a metal sipper tube will help keep the water clean. The sipper tube should be metal because guinea pigs sometimes chew and bite as they drink, and they can break glass sipper tubes.

Salt Spool Holder

In warmer weather, you should provide a salt spool for additional salt if your guinea pig needs it (see page 31). The salt spool is hung on the side of the cage. You can use wire to hold the salt spool, but be sure to use wire that won't rust. Metal shower curtain rings work well for this purpose. You can also purchase salt spool holders at feed stores or pet stores.

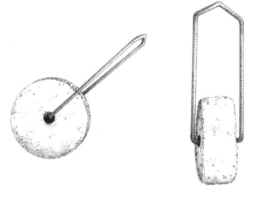

A salt spool on a holder, hung from the side of the cage, provides extra salt for your guinea pig in warm weather.

Privacy

To give a guinea pig a bit of privacy, provide a cardboard, wooden, or plastic box or a piece of PVC pipe. The box should be open on the bottom and one side. If

Guinea pig "houses" can be made of (clockwise,
from upper left): soft plastic, PVC pipe,
wood, and cardboard.

you add a little ramp, your guinea pig may like to climb
up to the top and sit there. Cardboard houses soil
quickly and need to be replaced often. Plastic houses
can be washed and reused. Wooden houses are reusable
but are harder to clean than PVC pipe or plastic houses.

Carpet Samples

Carpet samples come in handy when you are grooming,
examining, or showing your guinea pig. The carpet
provides good footing for the guinea pig and keeps it
from slipping. You can get carpet samples for free or at
low cost from a carpet store.

A small kitchen scale works well for weighing your guinea pig.

Grooming Tools

The grooming tools you need depend on the breed of guinea pig you have. See Chapter 6, "Grooming Your Guinea Pig," for the specific tools you need for each breed.

Scale

You need a scale for weighing your guinea pig. Weight is one way to check how well your guinea pig is growing. If you are going to show your guinea pig, you'll need to know how much it weighs in order to enter it in the correct show class.

Show Equipment

Carry Cage

If you will be taking your guinea pig to shows you will need a carry cage. A carry cage is a small travel cage, 8 inches by 8 inches by 8 inches tall or 10 inches by 10 inches by 8 inches tall. Like any guinea pig cage, it should have a solid floor. A carry cage is small to

A small pet carrier works well for transporting your guinea pig.

Caroline Kenyon transports her guinea pigs in a homemade wooden carry cage.

- A container for feed storage.

- A food dish or crock.

- A water bottle with a metal sipper tube.

- A salt spool holder.

- A small box or large PVC pipe for privacy.

- Carpet samples (for grooming and showing).

- Grooming tools (See "Grooming Your Guinea Pig," page 71).

- A scale.

- Show equipment.

- *Standard of Perfection.*

prevent injury while your guinea pig is in transit to and from a show. A small plastic pet carrier will work. You will need a small feed dish and a small water bottle for the carry cage.

It is a very good idea to have a blanket and/or sheet to cover the carry cage in cold weather or if there is a draft at the show.

Grooming/Show Table for Long-Haired Breeds

If you are showing long-haired breeds, you will need one or more special grooming tables for your intermediates and seniors (see page 26). These special grooming/show tables show off a long-haired breed's long coat to its best advantage.

Most breeders build their own grooming/show tables. A grooming/show table should measure 16 inches by 16 inches by 4 inches high. (Half-inch plywood works very well.) There should be handholds that are 4 inches long by 2 inches high in the middle of each side. The board should be covered with plain burlap cloth. You may also purchase grooming/show boards from mail-order rabbitry/caviary suppliers.

Standard of Perfection

If you plan to breed guinea pigs for show, you should have a copy of the *Standard of Perfection* (see page 11).

Long-haired breeds require a special show table.

Cleaning

Cleaning cages and all equipment is a very important part of keeping guinea pigs healthy. Trays, crocks, and water bottles should be scraped as clean as possible, rinsed with water, and dried before being placed back in the cage. Pipe cleaners work very well for scraping sipper tubes. Baby bottle brushes work well for scraping water bottles. Once a week, trays and all equipment should be washed thoroughly in soapy water and rinsed well. To dissolve urine deposits, soak trays in white vinegar for 20 minutes or so.

Once a month, all equipment should be sterilized. Wash your guinea pig's feed dish, water bottle, plastic or wooden house, and cage in soapy water and rinse them thoroughly. Then soak everything in a solution of one part bleach and ten parts water for 20 minutes, rinse thoroughly, and allow to dry in the sun. Spray the cage with the bleach solution, allow it to sit for 20 minutes, and then rinse thoroughly. A cage should be sterilized if an animal has been ill.

Important!

Do not use Lysol for cleaning your guinea pig's cage and equipment. It leaves a residue, even after rinsing, that can be toxic to guinea pigs.

Feeding Your Guinea Pig

Your guinea pig's health depends on a balanced diet that includes guinea pig feed pellets, fresh foods that provide vitamin C, alfalfa for protein and roughage, and fresh water. During warm weather, your guinea pig may need additional salt. And sometimes you'll want to offer your guinea pig a special treat.

Feed Pellets

Feed pellets made especially for guinea pigs are available at pet and feed stores. Guinea pig pellets are formulated to meet the particular nutritional needs of guinea pigs. Rabbit pellets do not have vitamin C, which is very important to a guinea pig's diet, and they also have too much of other vitamins that can cause illness in guinea pigs. The same is also true of mouse, rat, hamster, and other rodent foods. Unlike many other rodents, guinea pigs do not normally eat a lot of grains and seeds; seeds and grains are not good for them.

Your guinea pig's pellet dish or feeder should never be empty. Before you place pellets in the cage, use a small colander to sift out the fines, or dust.

Place the pellets at one end of the cage and the water at the other end of the cage so that your guinea

Guinea pig feed pellets are specially formulated for this animal's nutritional needs.

■ Do not use multiple
vitamins for humans
to add vitamin C to
your guinea pig's
diet. These may have
harmful ingredients
or may simply have
overdoses of vita-
mins that will make
your guinea pig ill.

■ If guinea pigs
receive a little more
vitamin C than they
actually need, it is
excreted in their
urine. Excessively
large amounts of
vitamin C, however,
can cause serious
kidney problems.

pig gets plenty of exercise walking between them.

If you use a pellet feeder, raise it 1–2 inches above
the cage floor to keep out feces and dirty bedding.

Store feed pellets in a cool, dry place. Throw away
any pellets that are over 90 days old since their nutritional value decreases with age.

Vitamin C

Your guinea pig has a very special dietary need —
vitamin C. Vitamin C is very important in keeping your
guinea pig healthy and in helping to fight off illness.
Guinea pigs do not manufacture vitamin C in their
bodies so they must get it in their diet.

Even though guinea pig pellets contain vitamin C,
its effectiveness is lost in a short time. Vitamin C is
destroyed by exposure to air, heat, light, and moisture
even when the best efforts have been taken to store it
properly. Therefore, it is very important to give your
guinea pig a fresh supply of vitamin C every day in
addition to its feed.

Guinea pigs need a minimum of 16 milligrams of
vitamin C per kilogram of body weight. Adult guinea
pigs weighing 2 to 4 pounds (1 to 2 kilograms) need a
minimum of 16 to 32 milligrams of vitamin C per day.
During times of stress — hot or cold weather, moving,
going to shows, breeding — guinea pigs need a few
extra milligrams of vitamin C per day because they use
it up quicker than when conditions are restful. The
same is true for growing pups and pregnant sows. For
example, you could give a growing pup weighing one
pound 10 to 12 milligrams of vitamin C, rather than
the minimum 8 milligrams per day.

Fresh Vegetables and Fruits

Washed fresh vegetables and fruits added to your
guinea pig's diet each day are an excellent source of the
necessary amount of vitamin C.

The following is a list of foods, with the correct amount of each, you can use to supplement your guinea pig's diet to ensure it gets enough vitamin C.

Vitamin C Requirements

Vegetable/Fruit	Amount Needed Each Day	
	2-Pound Guinea Pig requires 16 milligrams vitamin C	4-Pound Guinea Pig requires 32 milligrams vitamin C
Guavas	¼ ounce	½ ounce
Turnip greens	½ ounce	1 ounce
Kale leaves without stems	½ ounce	1 ounce
Parsley	½ ounce	1 ounce
Broccoli	¾ ounce	1½ ounces
Lemon with peel	¾ ounce	1½ ounces
Collard leaves	¾ ounce	1½ ounces
Orange with peel	1 ounce	2 ounces
Mustard greens	1 ounce	2 ounces
Spinach	1¼ ounces	2½ ounces
Strawberries	⅙ cup	⅓ cup

Crystallized Vitamin C

If you own a number of guinea pigs, you might prefer to purchase vitamin C in crystallized form that is made especially for guinea pigs. It is available by mail from rabbitry/caviary suppliers. (See "Helpful Sources," page 137.)

This crystallized form of vitamin C is placed in the guinea pigs' fresh drinking water daily, ⅛ to ¼ teaspoon of vitamin C per gallon of water.

Vitamin C ordered through the mail usually comes in larger amounts than you can use up quickly. It is a very good idea to place a small amount of your supply in a small, airtight container, such as a Tupperware midget 1- or 2-ounce container, for daily use. That way you won't be exposing your entire supply to the light and air every day. Keep all your vitamin C in airtight containers in a dark place in the refrigerator.

Water

Fresh water every day is as important as feed pellets and daily vitamin C. If a guinea pig does not have fresh water, it will not eat. A guinea pig that does not eat is soon a very sick guinea pig.

A plastic water bottle with a metal sipper tube is best for guinea pigs. The sipper tube should be metal and not glass because guinea pigs have a natural tendency to chew as they drink, and they can break a glass sipper tube. A sipper tube prevents a lot of germs that can make a guinea pig ill from getting into the water. The sipper tube should be rinsed thoroughly each time the bottle is refilled to get rid of any food that may have gotten into it when the guinea pig was drinking.

Alfalfa

Alfalfa is especially good for guinea pigs as a source of protein and roughage. Give your guinea pig fresh alfalfa at each cage cleaning, two or three times a week. Pet shops sell alfalfa in cubes — an alfalfa cube holder will help keep the alfalfa cubes clean and dry. Loose alfalfa may be purchased in small amounts from pet shops or by the bale at feed stores. It is a good idea to split a bale of alfalfa with friends so it does not get too old before it is used up. Try using a hay feeder or attaching the loose alfalfa to the side of the cage with a clothespin to keep it from getting soiled by droppings.

Store crystallized vitamin C in a small air-tight container with a proper label.

Alfalfa cubes are a good source of protein for your guinea pig.

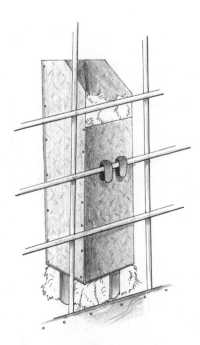

An alfalfa cube holder can be hung on
the inside of a wire cage.

Salt Spool

When the weather is very warm it is a good idea to
give your guinea pig a salt spool (see "Guinea Pig
Housing and Equipment," page 22). Your guinea
pig will decide if it needs the salt. Hang the salt
spool 1 to 2 inches above the floor of the cage
with a wire that won't rust or with a purchased
salt spool holder.

Special Treats

You can give your guinea pig small amounts of special
treats from time to time, but don't overdo it. Be careful
that its pellets and vitamin C sources remain the
majority of its diet.

If you feed treats in the morning, any treat left
should be removed from the cage at bedtime. Likewise,

Too many treats may
keep your guinea pig
from eating enough
pellets and vitamin C
sources to maintain
good health. Be
sparing with treats
and especially sparing
with *new* treats.

if you feed treats at night, remove any leftovers in the morning. This habit will keep the cage cleaner and prevent your guinea pig from eating spoiled food and getting sick.

For treats, guinea pigs like lettuce and other leafy green vegetables, such as kale, spinach, and celery. They also like carrots, apples, pears, grapes, berries, raisins, and yogurt-covered raisins. Apples are especially nice to use as a fluid source when you are traveling to and from shows and cannot use the water bottle. (Water bottles drip and get everything wet while traveling.) Carrots are also a good source of water, but a major drawback is that they turn your guinea pig's mouth orange.

Keeping Your Guinea Pig Healthy

Prevention

Prevention is the best medicine. Your guinea pig will be healthier and will be less expensive to care for if you take steps to prevent illness or other problems.

1. Keep your guinea pig's cage clean and dry.
2. Keep your guinea pig out of drafts.
3. Keep your guinea pig at a proper and constant temperature.
4. Make sure your guinea pig has plenty of fresh air.
5. Give your guinea pig fresh pellets and water daily.
6. Give your guinea pig a good source of vitamin C daily.
7. Give your guinea pig plenty of light (but not direct sunlight).
8. Keep your guinea pig's toenails clipped.
9. Examine your guinea pig often to find problems early.
10. Be very, very careful around your guinea pig if you have a cold or respiratory infection. You might

Always get the advice and assistance of your veterinarian before giving any kind of medical treatment to your guinea pig.

Warning!

Never! Never!! Never use any of the following with guinea pigs:

- Penicillin or any pen-icillin derivatives or synthetics. These are toxic to a guinea pig's digestive tract, resulting in death.

- Ampicillin.

- Ceclor.

- Keflex.

- Lincomycin.

- Spectinomycin.

- Carbenicillin.

- Erythromycin.

- Any product for dogs, cats, or other animals (flea pow-der, shampoo, etc.) that is not specifical-ly recommended for guinea pigs.

- Lysol, because it leaves a toxic residue even after being rinsed.

Call your veterinarian immediately if you do not feel comfortable doing a procedure.

wear a mask to protect your guinea pig from your cold. Keep your hands away from your face and keep your hands very clean when handling or working around your guinea pig. Keep your guinea pig away from your face.

11. Quarantine all new guinea pigs from your other stock. Keep them in a separate room if possible and handle them only after you are completely finished handling and caring for your other guinea pigs. This will prevent new stock from exposing your other guinea pigs to illness.

Before you begin working with a sick animal, gather all the items you think you will need. Be sure to wash your hands and wear examining gloves when dealing with infections, diarrhea, anal impaction, and other messy situations. When you are finished, clean up all the mess and dispose of it properly. Wash your hands!! This will help keep a sick guinea pig from getting sicker and prevent illness from spreading to healthy guinea pigs.

General Signs Of Illness

The sooner you spot any of these signs of illness and deal with them, the better chance your guinea pig has of recovering. These very general signs of illness may be present with any kind of illness. After you have noticed any of these signs, you need to determine the cause by checking the specific signs/symptoms of the diseases or conditions that are described below. The asterisk (*) means a condition is life threatening.

- Anorexia (not eating).*

- Not drinking.*

- Discharge from eyes and/or nose.*

- Diarrhea.*

- Hair loss.

- Weight loss.

- Dull, ruffled hair.

- Dull eyes, half-closed or closed eyes.

- Nose in corner of cage, hunched posture, not moving, listless.

Illnesses and Conditions

Abscess

Signs/symptoms: Hard lump under skin, may be warm to touch, hair loss on lump, may have appearance of a large pimple, may be open deep wound with drainage or discharge.

Cause: Bacterial infection in wound that does not drain properly, thus preventing healing.

Treatment:

1. Carefully remove hair over and surrounding the abscess.

2. Clean the surface on and around the abscess with an antiseptic scrub (such as Betadine Scrub).

3. Use a sterile lancet to carefully open the abscess.

4. Use a large syringe without a needle to flush the abscess with hydrogen peroxide, Betadine Scrub, or a mixture of the two until the abscess is completely clean.

5. Fill the abscess with Panolog Cream, Nolvasan Ointment, or other antibiotic ointment such as Neosporin.

6. Place warm, damp compresses on the abscess for 5 to 10 minutes, 2 to 3 times a day and reapply ointment.

7. Open the abscess (remove any scab) if necessary to clean and reapply ointment once a day until healed. This allows the abscess to heal from the inside.

Anal Impaction (occurs only in boars)

Signs/symptoms: Unpleasant odor, hardness felt in pouch between testicles, visible blockage of anal pouch.
Cause: Not well understood but thought to be caused by lack of bulk or fiber in diet. The anal pouch is naturally sticky, so may pick up bedding or other material that sticks in the pouch.
Treatment: You may want to wear a dust mask with a few drops of perfume the first few times you do this until you learn to catch the problem before the odor is terrible.

1. Wear rubber gloves.

2. Do not ever pull the blockage or lump out of the pouch. You may seriously injure your boar.

3. Soak the pouch area in lukewarm, soapy water or soften the blockage with mineral oil or vitamin E oil.

4. Beginning at the outside edge of the blockage use mineral oil, baby oil, or KY Jelly on a cotton swab to gently remove the blockage from the skin and the pouch.

5. Once the blockage is removed, use a syringe without a needle to flush the pouch as clean as possible with warm soapy water.

6. Examine the pouch carefully for infection (redness, swelling, pus) or sores. If there are no sores or infection, apply Panolog Cream or petroleum jelly thoroughly inside the pouch. If there are sores or infection, apply antibiotic ointment (such as Neosporin, Tribiotic, or Bacitracin). Apply Panolog Cream as protection and as a lubricant.

7. Examine the anal pouch at least once a week. Clean the pouch as needed to prevent a blockage buildup.

Broken Bones

Signs/symptoms: Limping, not moving, swelling, localized pain, noticeable distortion of body part.
Cause: Falling, injury due to wire floor, incorrect handling.
Treatment: See veterinarian. Keep the animal as still and comfortable as possible.

Broken Front Teeth

Signs/symptoms: Missing, chipped, or loose teeth.
Cause: Wire chewing, falling, scurvy.
Treatment:

1. Use toenail clippers or tooth nippers to trim chipped teeth even.

2. Feed soft foods and wet pellets.

3. When tooth is no longer loose or the missing tooth is beginning to grow back, give a block of pinewood for chewing. The tooth should grow back in a week or so if it has not been damaged too severely.

4. Make sure guinea pig gets proper nutrition, especially vitamin C.

Bumblefoot

Signs/symptoms: Noticeable reddening on the sole of the foot with noticeable swelling, sores on sole of foot that open and bleed.
Cause: Wire floors, possible scratches from splinters in wood shavings, dirty cage floor causing irritation to sole of foot.
Treatment: Treatment may not be effective. If condition doesn't improve after following these steps, see your veterinarian.

1. Change to solid floor if using wire floors.

2. Examine wood shavings for splinters that could cause an injury to feet.

3. Keep floor very clean.

4. Trim nails short.

5. If foot is only showing redness, rub Bag Balm on foot as needed (once or twice a day) until redness is gone.

6. Clean wounds with hydrogen peroxide or Betadine Scrub.

7. Apply Panolog Ointment to foot and bandage foot. Do not make bandage too tight.

8. Change bandage daily and reapply Panolog Ointment.

9. If the foot hasn't healed after 5 to 7 days of this treatment, take the guinea pig to the veterinarian.

Cloudy Eye

Signs/symptoms: Cloudy film over eye of newborn guinea pig.
Cause: The turning in of the eyelid, which causes a scratch on the cornea, resulting in a cloudy film.
Treatment: Cut or puncture a vitamin A or vitamin E capsule and squeeze one drop into eye twice daily until eye is clear. Or use Terramycin ophthalmic ointment twice daily.

Colds, Pneumonia, and Respiratory Infections

Signs/symptoms: Discharge from eyes, nose, or both, sneezing, coughing, difficulty breathing (you may hear or feel a rattle in chest), backbone may appear to stick out, dehydration (lift loose skin to see if it stands up instead of falling flat and tight on the body).

Cause: Drafts, viral or bacterial infection, stress, poor ventilation that allows buildup of harmful ammonia levels.

Treatment: Isolate animal.

1. Give Albon liquid, 240 milligrams per teaspoon, .5 milliliters per pound of weight, twice daily. (A 2-pound cavy would take 1 milliliter.) Treat for 5 days. If no response, see veterinarian for a stronger antibiotic. (See page 139.)

2. For herd treatment of directly exposed animals (animals in same cage or only separated by wire): Give tetracycline or oxytetracycline powder, 1 tablespoon per gallon of water. Keep water out of sunlight, and change daily. Or give Sulmet or Sulfa Nox in drinking water, 1 tablespoon per gallon of water.

3. Treat for 7 days or until symptoms are gone. Evaluate effectiveness of treatment at 5 days. If no improvement, see your veterinarian.

4. If your guinea pig is shivering or seems cold, heat half of the cage with a light bulb or set half of the cage on a heating pad set to low.

5. Increase vitamin C to maximum of 50 milligrams per day (several small doses over the day so as not to overwork the kidneys).

6. Force fluids by mouth with eyedropper or syringe without needle every half hour. See "Fluids," below.

7. Force feed between fluids every hour. See Feed, below. Continue until guinea pig is able to eat on its own.

8. Put a decongestant rub (such as Vicks VapoRub) around nose and under chin to help open airways and make breathing easier. Do not put in nostrils.

9. Place 3 to 5 drops of a mild nasal decongestant (such as Neo-Synephrine Nose Drops ¼%) in clogged nose as needed. (The further apart the doses of the decongestant, the better.)

> **Caution:**
>
> Do not mix vitamin C into water when using antibiotics in water. The vitamin C will be destroyed or the antibiotic will be ineffective.

10. If animal is still having trouble breathing after using the decongestant rub, then spray 2 to 3 puffs of a bronchodilator (bronchial mist for asthma) in the face close to the nose. Cover eyes to protect from spray. Use every 2 to 6 hours as needed for difficult breathing. (The further apart the bronchial mist treatments, the better.)

Fluids for Treatment of Colds

One to three of these fluids every half hour. Give as much as you can get the animal to take by eyedropper or syringe without needle.

- Vitamin C water (regular drinking water).

- A mixture of 1 part vegetable juice drink, 1 part water, 1 part light corn syrup.

- Orange juice.

- Puppy or kitten milk replacer.

- Sugar water (1 tablespoon light corn syrup in 4 ounces water).

- Acidophilus water (¼ to ½ acidophilus capsule in 8 ounces of water).

Unused fluids should be discarded every 24 hours and made up fresh as needed.

Feeds for Treatment of Colds

Mix together 1 jar carrot baby food, 2 jars broccoli and chicken baby food (you may use any vegetable-chicken or vegetable-turkey combination), 2 tablespoons light corn syrup, 3 tablespoons high-protein baby cereal, 1 jar baby orange juice, 1 capsule acidophilus. Add enough water so mixture can be given with an eyedropper or syringe without needle. This mixture may be frozen in ice cube trays, then stored in freezer bags in the freezer until needed, usually 1 or 2 cubes of feed are used per day. The feed may need to be thinned after it is thawed. Or mix together 1 part kitten milk replacer, 2 parts water, 1 part broccoli and chicken baby food. (You may use any vegetable-chicken or vegetable-turkey combination.) Both of these mixtures should be stored in the refrigerator while in use and warmed slightly so as to be room temperature or slightly warmer before feeding. (Hold full eyedropper or syringe without needle under hot water or in a glass of hot water for 1 to 2 minutes.) Feed as much as you can get the animal to take each hour.

Caution:

Check expiraton dates on all medications and discard old medications.

Conjunctivitis (Eye Infection)

Signs/symptoms: Cloudy film over eye, redness, swelling, may have discharge, eye may be stuck closed.
Cause: Bacterial infection, irritation or injury from bedding or dust.
Treatment:
1. If eye is stuck closed, carefully moisten eye and clean area so eye can be opened.

2. Place Terramycin ophthalmic ointment from your veterinarian or the feed store in eye 2 to 3 times daily until eye is clear. Or place triple antibiotic (Bacitracin-Neomycin-Polymyxin) ophthalmic ointment in eye 2 to 3 times daily until eye is clear.

3. You may also give, along with the antibiotic, a half capsule of vitamin A in the eye 1 to 2 times daily.

Constipation

Signs/symptoms: Very dry, hard droppings, no droppings.
Cause: Lack of water, lack of greens.
Treatment:
1. Feed apple peel and watch for normal droppings. Or use 2 drops olive oil on pellets or by mouth and watch for normal droppings.

2. Add more greens to diet as needed.

Diarrhea

Signs/symptoms: Loose, watery stools, appears healthy otherwise.

Cause: Too many greens, possible viral infection, parasites, breakdown of the natural bacteria in digestive tract.

Treatment:

1. Clean cages and equipment and change bedding daily.

2. Remove or limit greens in diet until condition improves.

3. Feed grass hay only until diarrhea is gone.

4. Boil drinking water until diarrhea is gone.

5. Give live culture yogurt or acidophilus in water (¼ to ½ acidophilus capsule in 8 ounces of water) by eyedropper or syringe without needle by mouth until diarrhea is gone.

6. If above remedies are ineffective, feed rice water or dry, uncooked oatmeal or rice cereal. Give in small amounts and decrease the amount as stools return to normal.

If guinea pig still has diarrhea after 4 to 6 hours with the above treatments, try the following:

7. Give pediatric electrolyte maintenance solution (such as Pedialyte) or Nop Stress in drinking bottle (8 ounces) next to regular drinking water bottle to replace fluids lost from diarrhea.

8. ¼ teaspoon anti-diarrhea medicine (such as Kaopectate) by spoon or eyedropper 3 to 4 times a day, decrease dose as stool returns to normal. Or use Dry Tail, following instructions on package.

If your guinea pig does not seem to be responding to the above treatment after one day, take it to your veterinarian. (See page 139.) Take a sample of the guinea pig's stool so the veterinarian can check for parasites.

Hair Loss (Barbering)

Signs/symptoms: Hair cropped or trimmed irregularly, may be cropped very close to skin. Hair appears healthy, skin appears normal without dandruff.
Cause: Barbering or chewing hair by the guinea pig or its cage mates.
Treatment:
1. Separate animals if caged together.
2. Try giving extra hay or alfalfa to chew.

Hair Loss (Alopecia)

Signs/symptoms: General or patchy loss of hair, skin appears normal without dandruff, may be seen in pregnant sows.
Cause: Unknown, possibly vitamin C deficiency, possibly dietary deficiency, parasites.
Treatment:
1. Nutritionally balanced diet recommended.
2. Be certain animal is getting enough vitamin C (minimum 16 milligrams per kilogram weight daily, slightly more if stressed). (See "Mites.")

Alopecia is the cause of this sow's hair loss.

Heatstroke

Signs/symptoms: Drooling, rapid breathing, weakness, listlessness, blood-tinged discharge from nose and mouth, increased water intake, sunken eyes, bony over rump, unconscious.
Cause: Surrounding temperature over 75° Fahrenheit with high humidity of 70 percent or above, exposure to direct sun, crowding, lack of water.
Treatment:
1. Spray with water via spray bottle set on fine mist.
2. Dip in water, starting with a temperature of luke-

warm and slowly add cold tap water to decrease the temperature of the water, causing the guinea pig's body temperature to decrease slowly.

3. Force fluids only if guinea pig is conscious (awake and able to swallow): Gatorade, sugar water (preferably of light corn syrup, 1 tablespoon dissolved in 4 ounces of water), Pedialyte (or equivalent), Nop Stress, or Vitapol (1 teaspoon in 1 gallon of water), vitamin C water. Give as much as you can get the animal to take by eyedropper or syringe without needle every half hour. Force-feed if necessary. (See treatment for colds.)

4. After following above procedure, immediately take guinea pig to veterinarian for further treatment. (See page 140.)

Lice

Signs/symptoms: Scratching, severe hair loss, *dermatitis, pruritus,* skin thickened, dry, scaly, scabby sores; lice may be seen around ears and rump.
Cause: Tiny parasites brought in on bedding or spread by infected guinea pigs.
Treatment: Separate infected animals from noninfected animals; treat all as if infected.

1. Clean cage thoroughly.

2. Dip guinea pigs in pyrethrin dip. Follow label directions. (Wear rubber gloves and do not breathe the fumes.) Be sure to carefully rub the dip on the head with your hands. Do not get dip in eyes, ears, nose, or mouth of the animal. Or bathe in Mycodex shampoo with pyrethrins. Repeat bath with Mycodex shampoo 1 week later. Dry the guinea pig with a blow-dryer on warm setting. Keep the dryer 6 inches away from the guinea pig so it does not become overheated. Or keep the guinea pig in a warm, draft-free room until dry. Examine your guinea pig in 2 weeks and repeat the dip if necessary.

Malocclusion
(Misalignment of Front Teeth)

Signs/symptoms: Bottom front teeth in front of top front teeth, front teeth very long and curling inward or outward or both. Mouth may not open if teeth are locked together because of curling.

Cause: Heredity, falling, wire chewing.

Treatment:

1. Use toenail clippers, wire cutters, or tooth nippers to trim teeth even as needed, at 2- to 3-week intervals. (Sometimes it is necessary to trim down to the gum line. Your guinea pig can still chew and eat with its molars.)

2. Give pinewood block for chewing.

3. Do not use this animal for breeding if you know this condition is *congenital* (from birth, inherited).

4. Watch for infection of the teeth and gums.

Mites: Fur

Signs/symptoms: Scratching, hair loss possibly in the shape of a V on the back or belly, scaly skin.

Cause: Tiny parasites brought in on bedding or spread by an infected guinea pig.

Treatment:

1. Separate infected animals from noninfected animals. Treat all as if infected.

2. Clean cage thoroughly.

3. Sprinkle floor and bedding with cat flea powder or spray with a pyrethrin flea spray. Do not get powder or spray in eyes, ears, mouth, or nose of the animal.

4. Sprinkle cat flea powder on guinea pigs or spray with a pyrethrin flea spray.

Congenital. *Present from birth.*

5. Follow above instructions for 2 to 3 weeks, each time the cage is cleaned.

Mites: Skin

Signs/symptoms: Scratching, severe hair loss, dermatitis, pruritus, skin thickened, dry, scaly, scabby sores.
Cause: Tiny parasites brought in on bedding or spread by infected guinea pigs.
Treatment: Separate infected animals from noninfected animals; treat all as if infected.

1. Clean cage thoroughly.

2. Dip guinea pigs in a pyrethrin dip. Follow label directions. (Wear rubber gloves and do not breathe the fumes.) Be sure to carefully rub the dip on the head with your hands. Do not get dip in eyes, ears, nose, or mouth of the animal. Or bathe in Mycodex shampoo with pyrethrins. Repeat with Mycodex shampoo bath 1 week later.

3. Blow-dry the guinea pig with a blow-dryer on warm setting. Keep dryer 6 inches away from your guinea pig so it does not become overheated.

4. Examine guinea pig in 2 weeks and repeat dip if necessary.

5. Instead of above treatment, give ivermectrin (0.02 milliliters per pound of weight). Give by mouth with eyedropper or syringe without needle. Or mix 1 milliliter ivomec 1% with 10 milliliters fruit-flavor baby food and give 0.2 milliliters per pound of body weight. Discard unused portion.

6. Repeat ivermectrin application at 2 to 3 weeks and then as necessary.

Mites: Ear

Signs/symptoms: Shaking head, scratching head and ears, dirty, reddish brown "wax" inside ear.

Cause: Tiny parasite brought in on bedding or spread by infected guinea pigs.

Treatment:

1. Separate infected animals from noninfected animals (keep a close watch on noninfected animals).

2. Clean ears gently with cotton swabs and a tiny amount of alcohol.

3. Fill ear canal with a miticide for cats twice daily for 2 weeks, or longer if necessary, until reddish brown "wax" is gone, and ear stays clean.

Pea Eye

Signs/symptoms: A lump in the lower eyelid, not an abscess.

Cause: A hereditary condition in which the ligaments holding fatty tissue below the eyelid break down, causing the build-up of fatty tissue in the lower eyelid.

Treatment: None. Do not use this animal for breeding because this condition is hereditary and will be passed on to offspring.

Polydactyl

Signs/symptoms: Having an extra toe or toes on the feet.

Cause: Heredity.

Treatment: None. Do not use this animal for breeding because this condition is hereditary.

Penis Problems (boars only)

Signs/symptoms: Penis is stiff, dry, inflamed, or may have hair wrapped around it. Bedding materials may be stuck to penis and sheath; may be gelatin-like discharge from penis.

Cause: Dirty cage.

Treatment: Never pull off anything that is stuck to the penis or sheath. You may seriously injure your boar.

1. Soak penis and sheath in mild soapy water until anything that is stuck comes off easily.

2. If necessary use mineral oil or baby oil and cotton swabs to carefully clean the penis and sheath.

3. Apply Panolog Cream or petroleum jelly to penis and sheath as needed until healed or appearance returns to normal.

Pregnancy Toxemia

See "Breeding Your Guinea Pigs," page 62.

Ringworm

Signs/symptoms: Bald patches, usually beginning on nose and face then spreading to abdomen and back, skin may be a little dry and/or scaly or crusty.
Cause: Fungus.
Treatment:

1. Isolate guinea pig.

2. Wear rubber gloves and clean cage and equipment thoroughly.

3. Wear rubber gloves and clean affected areas on guinea pig with cotton and warm, soapy water. Dry the area and all the surrounding areas well. Gently remove any crust.

4. Rub Tinactin 3% sulfur ointment into area and surrounding hair 1 to 2 times daily. (Clean the area thoroughly before each application of Tinactin.) Continue until hair is growing back.

5. If fungus persists, see veterinarian for alternative treatment. (See page 140.)

Scurvy

Signs/symptoms: Hair loss, weight loss, loss of coordination, loose teeth, bleeding gums, swollen and painful joints, listless, unthrifty (see page 135), dehydration

> Ringworm can be transmitted to humans from guinea pigs.

(lift loose skin to see if it stands up instead of falling flat and tight on the body).
Cause: Lack of vitamin C.
Treatment: Do not use a multivitamin product that could cause potential toxic overdose of other vitamins!

Give vitamin C up to 50 milligrams per day in water and/or greens until signs and symptoms are gone. Divide the vitamin C into several small doses over the day so as not to overwork the kidneys.

Slobbers

Signs/symptoms: Slobbering, drooling, weight loss, mouth does not close all the way.
Cause: Overgrown molars possibly due to lack of chewing or hereditary malocclusion of molars.
Treatment: See veterinarian. Molars may need to be filed as needed. Do not use this animal for breeding because this condition may be hereditary and could be passed on to offspring.

Sores and Wounds

Signs/symptoms: Open wound or scratch.
Cause: Fighting if overcrowded or incompatible, injury from unsafe cage or surroundings.
Treatment:
1. Trim hair around wound.
2. Clean wound with antiseptic soap.
3. Apply Panolog Cream or apply topical antibiotic ointment (such as Neosporin).

Vaginal Infection (sows only)

Signs/Symptoms: White mucous discharge with or without odor from genital area.
Cause: Dirty cage, bacterial infection, may get infected from boar not kept clean, fat or older animals not able to clean themselves.

Treatment:

1. Disinfect cage.

2. Force fluids and feed if guinea pig is not drinking and eating. (See treatment for colds, page {00}.)

Wry Neck: Torticollis

Signs/Symptoms: Head held at tilt to one side, may stagger and/or fall over when walking.
Cause: Infection in middle or inner ear.
Treatment: Head may remain tilted if the infection causes severe damage to the ear, but otherwise the guinea pig will be normal.

For veterinarian's treatment, see page 140.

Wry Neck: In Newborn

Signs/symptoms: Head tilts to one side, may stagger and/or fall over when walking.
Cause: Birth presentation or position in the uterus before born.
Treatment: None. If not severe, this condition will correct itself in 3 to 4 days. Watch to see if newborn can nurse. You may be able to help feed a newborn that cannot nurse, but if the condition is too severe, you will not be able to do anything, and the guinea pig will probably die.

Guinea Pig First-Aid Kit

The following is a list of items you should try to have on hand as a first-aid kit in case your guinea pig becomes ill or has a problem. The letters in parentheses tell you where you should be able to find the listed item: D-Drug store, G-Grocery store, V-Veterinarian, F-Feed store, P-Pet store, or H-Health food store.

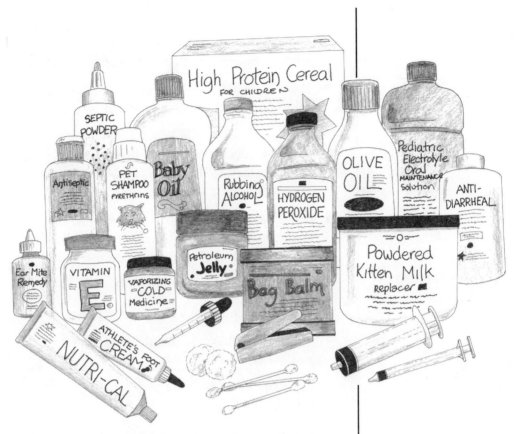

These are the ingredients that should be included in a guinea pig first-aid kit.

- Your veterinarian's phone number.

- Latex examining gloves (D,V) — Wear to protect you and help keep problem area clean.

- Cotton balls/cotton swabs (D,G) — Treating anal impaction, cleaning wounds and ears.

- Plastic eyedropper (V) — Feeding sick animals or newborn pups, administering medications.

- Bottles with eyedroppers (V,D) — Storing food or medication being used at a particular time.

- Syringes without needles (V,F) — Feeding sick animals, administering medication, flushing wounds.

- Heating pad (D) — Warming a sick guinea pig. (Always set on "Low" and cover pad with a towel to prevent burning.)

- Mild nasal decongestant drops (such as Neo-Synephrine Nose Drops ¼%) (D) — Treating a guinea pig with a stuffy nose.

- Bronchodilator spray (such as Primatene Mist or Bronkaid Mist) (D,G) — Treating a guinea pig with difficult breathing as with pneumonia.

- Bag Balm (F) — Treating bumblefoot.

- Hydrogen peroxide 3% (D,G) — Treating wounds.

- Tinactin 3% sulfur ointment (V) — Treating ringworm.

- Styptic powder (Kwick Stop or Nik Stop) (P,F) — To stop bleeding.

- Miticide Liquid for cats (V,P,F) — Treating ear mites.

- Panolog ointment or cream (V) — Treating minor cuts, scrapes, anal impaction, penis problems, abscesses.

- Nutri-Cal (P,F) — Feeding newborn guinea pigs, making feed for ill guinea pigs.

- Baby food (G) — Making feed for ill guinea pigs.

- Kitten or puppy milk replacer (V,F,P) — Feeding orphan pups, making feed for ill guinea pigs.

- Mycodex shampoo (F,P,V) — Treating mites.

- Acidophilus (live culture), live culture yogurt (G,H) — Replacing digestive tract bacteria lost with diarrhea.

- Anti-diarrhea medicine (such as Kaopectate) (D,G) — Treating diarrhea.

- Dry Tail (P) — Treating diarrhea.

- Olive oil (G,H) — Treating constipation.

- Pyrethrin flea powder or lice powder or spray or dip (V,F,P) — Treating fur mites or lice.

- Ivermectrin (V,F) — Treating mites, worms.

- Petroleum jelly (D,G) — Lubricant.

- Medicated chest rub decongestant (such as Vick's VapoRub) (D,G) — To ease breathing and congestion.

- Gatorade/pediatric electrolyte maintenance solution (such as Pedialyte) (D,G) — For water replacement after dehydration.

- Nop Stress, Vitapol (F) — For water replacement after dehydration.

- Vitamin A/vitamin E capsules (H,G,D) — Treating cloudy eye in newborn or infection of eye.

- Rubbing alcohol (D,G) — Cleaning ears, wounds.

- Children's C-Vi-Sol/Poly-Vi-Sol (D,G) — Treating travel stress.

- Baby oil (D,G) — Cleaning anal pouch, scaly ears.

- Vitamin C (H,G, Mail Order) — Preventing scurvy.

- Antiseptic scrub (such as Betadine Scrub) (D,F,V) — Cleaning wounds.

- Terramycin powder (F,V) — Drug of choice for treating early stages of pneumonia, diarrhea, crusty eyes.

- Sulmet, Sulfa Nox (F,V) — Drug of choice for treating respiratory infection, eye infection, first signs of cold.

- Tetracycline (fish antibiotic) (P,V) — Treating infections and lung ailments.

- Baytril (V) — Drug of choice for treating pneumonia.

- Pill splitter (D) — For breaking medication tablets.

- Pill crusher (D) — For crushing vitamin C tablets.

- Small piller (V) — For giving pills without being bitten.

Breeding Your Guinea Pigs

The Purpose of Breeding

The purpose of breeding is to improve your guinea pigs. Maybe you want to improve the health and eye appeal of your pet guinea pigs. Maybe you want to breed for better show-quality guinea pigs. Whatever the reason, breeding should be done very carefully.

Guinea pigs that look unhealthy but have no apparent signs or symptoms of illness are called *unthrifty*. Breeding unthrifty guinea pigs does not improve the health or appearance of future generations. A fault is something that detracts from the appearance of a guinea pig so that the guinea pig is not perfect. Small eyes or narrow shoulders are examples of faults. Breeding guinea pigs with the same faults does not improve show stock because their offspring are likely to inherit the faults. You should evaluate your breeding stock carefully in order to achieve the best possible outcome from a breeding.

Choosing Guinea Pigs for Breeding

Your decision about which guinea pigs to breed together should be based on the characteristics that you want the offspring to inherit.

Inbreeding

Inbreeding is breeding two very closely related guinea pigs: mother to son, daughter to father, brother to sister. Sometimes inbreeding is done when the parent and offspring or siblings have exceptionally outstanding desirable characteristics, and the breeder wishes to make these characteristics stronger. If a characteristic is strong, it will occur in offspring more often than not. Inbreeding may also make bad characteristics stronger, so it must be done with great care.

Line Breeding

Line breeding is breeding guinea pigs with a common ancestor: guinea pigs that have the same father but different mothers or the same mother but different fathers; cousins that have the same grandfather or grandmother. Again, as with inbreeding, the breeder is trying to make certain characteristics appear more often in the offspring.

Outcrossing or Outbreeding

Outcrossing or *outbreeding* is breeding totally unrelated guinea pigs. Outbreeding may cause some drastic changes in the characteristics of the offspring. Outbreeding may be necessary if the offspring from breedings of related animals begin to show some weakness, such as not making weight.

Breeding Warning

It is not a good idea to breed a roan boar to a roan sow or vice versa. Roan is the color generated by the intermingling of white hair with any other color (see page 8). Breeding roan to roan can cause a fatal gene combination. A pup that has inherited this gene is usually smaller than its litter mates, white in color, and the eyes are set wrong (they are rotated in the wrong direction). They are often blind, deaf, and have crooked or no teeth. These offspring are very unthrifty and usually die shortly after birth.

When to Breed

Guinea pigs can be bred year-round. Sows should be at least 4 months of age and weigh a minimum of 22 ounces before being introduced to a boar for breeding. Be very careful not to breed a sow before she meets these requirements.

On the other hand, a sow that is over 1 year old and has never had a litter should not be bred. This is because a sow's pelvic bones fuse together at around the age of 1 year if she hasn't given birth. The pelvic bones will not separate to allow young to be born, resulting in the death of both the sow and the litter.

Boars may reproduce as early as 8 weeks of age, but it is a good idea to let them mature to at least 16 weeks (4 months) of age before using them for breeding.

A sow can be used for breeding up to around ages 3 to 4 and a boar up to around ages 4 to 5. After these ages, pregnancy may occur less often, and litter size may decrease markedly. Generally as a sow ages, each pregnancy carries more risk of problems.

Preparing for Breeding

Nutrition

Plan ahead. Use diet and nutrition to prepare your sow for breeding well ahead of the actual time of mating. Make sure she does not get fat, because being overweight may cause *infertility* or increase the risk of pregnancy toxemia.

Introduce the sow to the foods you want her to have during pregnancy: bits of carrot for vitamin K to decrease bleeding at the time of delivery, bits of broccoli for vitamin C to meet the sow's increased need for

It is very dangerous for a sow and her litter if she is bred when she is too young and physically immature.

Something to Consider

Before you breed your guinea pigs, you need to consider what will happen to the offspring. It is very irresponsible to breed your guinea pigs without a definite plan for finding homes for the offspring.

- Do friends want some or all of the offspring?

- Can you sell to local pet stores?

- Can you sell showable animals?

- If things change and you can't find homes for them all, do you have enough cages for your new guinea pigs?

Recipe for Sugar Water

1 tablespoon light corn syrup in 4 ounces water.

Breeding Cage Size Requirements

- For 1 boar and 1 sow: 24" x 24"

- For 1 boar and 5 sows: 36" x 36"

vitamin C, and calcium to help with contractions during delivery. Make sure she is familiar with sugar water and Gatorade. Try giving her ½ to 1 teaspoon Calf-Manna or COB (corn-oats-barley) with molasses to add protein and high-energy sugars to her diet. These last two items may cause diarrhea, so be cautious. If the sow eats and drinks these things before she is pregnant, she will not hesitate to eat or drink them when she is pregnant and needs them the most.

Also prepare the boar for breeding by making sure he is not too fat, which can cause sterility. Make sure that he is in the best of health.

Special Preparations for Long-Haired Breeds

If you are breeding long-haired Silkies or Peruvians, you will need to cut the boar's and sow's hair short, especially around the rump. Long hair gets in the way of mating and may get tangled around a boar's penis, causing severe problems.

The Breeding Cage

Prepare the breeding cage in advance. A top-opening cage is easy to clean without having to handle the pregnant sow during the last 2 to 3 weeks of her pregnancy. Place food at one end of the cage and water at the other end to make sure the boar and sow get good exercise.

Place the boar in the breeding cage by himself 1 or 2 days before you introduce the sow.

More than One Sow, One Boar

If you are a breeder, you may decide to breed more than one sow to the same boar. As a general rule you can place as many as five sows with a single boar for breeding. If you will be breeding more than one sow to one boar, place these sows together in another cage for 1 or 2 days to make sure they all get along. Watch the sows closely after you put them together. There may be a little mild fighting or disagreement at first, but it should stop after a few minutes without injury to any of them.

One Sow, One Boar

Placing one sow with one boar for breeding makes things a bit easier on the sow for these reasons:

A single sow can remain in the breeding cage from mating through delivery and weaning. When several sows are with a boar, each sow will need to be moved to a new cage for delivery. This may increase stress and therefore in-crease the risk of pregnancy toxemia. Note, however, that it is better to move a sow at the end of her preg-nancy than in the middle of her pregnancy.

Sometimes, when one sow goes into labor, other pregnant sows around her also go into labor, even if they aren't at the end of their pregnancies. If these sows deliver too prematurely, their litters will not survive.

Putting Sows and Boars Together

After you are satisfied the sows are compatible (if you are breeding more than one), and the boar has become accustomed to his cage, introduce the sow or sows to the boar in his cage. Again watch for any prolonged fighting between sows or between sows and boar. Do not allow prolonged fighting of any kind to continue.

At this time, add a second drinking bottle, a small 8-ounce size with orange-flavored Gatorade or sugar

Sows that fight nonstop and appear unable to settle their differences with the others should be removed from the group. You may try again to introduce these sows to the group at a later time.

It is best to place the sow in the boar's cage for mating. A sow may be protective of her own cage and fight with the boar rather than breed to him.

water next to the regular drinking bottle. The Gatorade or sugar water will give the sow extra sugars that are easy to digest and that provide extra energy if she needs it. Change the Gatorade and wash drinking bottles daily.

You may also increase the amount of vitamin C for each guinea pig by a few milligrams. They will use a lot of energy and vitamin C while breeding. The sow will use a lot of vitamin C during and after pregnancy, so it may be increased slightly throughout the pregnancy and up to the time the pups are weaned.

Mating

A guinea pig sow comes into *estrus* or *heat* every 15 to 17 days. Estrus lasts only 24 to 48 hours. During this time, she will be receptive to a boar and able to *conceive* — become pregnant — if mating occurs. You can tell if a sow is ready for mating by touching her on the back. If she is ready to accept a boar for breeding, she will lower her back and slightly raise her rump.

Gestation

Guinea pigs may be bred year-round. A sow's *gestation* period is 63 to 72 days. Gestation is the period of time from conception (when a sow actually becomes pregnant) to delivery (when a sow gives birth to her offspring). You may never actually see your guinea pigs breed or mate, so you may never know exactly when a sow is due to deliver.

On rare occasions, a sow may become pregnant, then have an estrus cycle 2 weeks later and conceive a second litter. Very rarely, this sow will deliver the first litter and then 2 weeks later deliver the second litter. What is more likely to happen is that

Estrus, heat. *The period when a sow can become pregnant.*

Conceive. *Become pregnant.*

Gestation. *The time from conception to birth.*

A sow with a large litter may have a slightly shorter pregnancy than if she were carrying a normal size litter.

Introduced   12-01-94

122   Kandy Korn

PSC68   Rhion

A breeding card identifies the names and numbers of the
sow and boar and the date they were put together.

both litters will be delivered when the first litter is due.
The smaller, premature litter will usually not be able to
survive.

Write the sow's and boar's names and ear tag
numbers on the calendar under the date that they were
introduced. You should also place a small card on the
cage with the date and the names and identification
numbers of the guinea pigs. (You also may use a special
notebook for these records.)

To improve the chances for the sow to become
pregnant, keep the boar with the sow for at least 32
days or the equivalent of two of the sow's estrus cycles.
You can leave the boar with the sow, to provide company, through the eighth week of pregnancy.

Both the boar and the sow will make cooing noises
and purr during their courtship. The boar will mount
the sow over her rump to mate. After the sow becomes
pregnant, the boar will not try to mate with her again.
This is usually the first clue that your sow is pregnant.

Causes of Pregnancy Toxemia

Pregnancy toxemia is thought to be caused by a wide combination of things, including:

- Sow too young or too old

- Sow too fat or too thin

- Excessive heat

- Sow does not eat or diet does not provide enough energy

- Stress

- All of the above

Pregnancy Toxemia

Sows need extra attention during pregnancy to prevent a serious illness called *pregnancy toxemia.* If a sow uses more energy than she is taking in through her diet, she must get the energy she needs by *metabolizing* her own fat. This causes ketone bodies and acid buildup in her blood. This is pregnancy toxemia, and it makes a pregnant sow very ill. The problem may also occur after the sow has delivered her litter.

Cause

The actual cause of pregnancy toxemia is not really understood. It is considered to be linked to how the guinea pig's body uses food or breaks down food for use by the body. So by being very careful with a sow's diet before, during, and after pregnancy, you can reduce the risk of pregnancy toxemia quite a bit.

Keeping stress to a minimum also helps reduce the risk of pregnancy toxemia. Do not change a pregnant sow's cage, feed, regular habits, or the temperature or lighting in her environment. Do not introduce new cage mates into a pregnant sow's cage. And while a sow can produce as many as six litters a year, breeding that often may increase a sow's risk of pregnancy toxemia.

Signs of Pregnancy Toxemia

The signs and symptoms of pregnancy toxemia are basically not eating or drinking. You should also be concerned if you notice your sow seeming to suddenly drink very large amounts of water as opposed to her usual amount per day. This may be a sign of ketone bodies and acid building up in the sow's blood.

Treatment

Treatment of pregnancy toxemia means a trip to the veterinarian for administration of lactated Ringer's solution, calcium gluconate, 5% glucose, and more. The veterinarian may give a shot of oxytocin to start or help a sow's labor or may perform a *Caesarean section.* Treatment is not always successful, so prevention is best.

Early Pregnancy

Around the fourth to fifth week of pregnancy you should notice your sow becoming more and more pear shaped. Her sides should feel fairly solid rather than soft and flaccid. About 3 weeks before she is due to deliver, you may start seeing the pups kick. At this time, you need to stop handling your sow (actually picking up and moving her around). You will notice that your sow seems more and more uncomfortable. She will seem agitated or restless; she may move around her cage and form a "race track." You may notice that she is chewing and/or eating more shavings or bedding materials.

Late Pregnancy

Approximately 2 weeks before she gives birth, the sow's pelvic bones begin to *dilate* or separate. If you have not removed the boar before this time, do so now. Your sow will begin to appear to drag her belly on the floor when she walks. She will also look as if she has a caboose on her rump due to the separation of the pelvic bones. If you touch the area just in front of the genital area very gently and carefully, you will be able to feel the space between the pelvic bones. When the space between the bones is about as wide as a finger (approximately 15 millimeters), your sow will probably deliver in about 24 hours.

Carefully check your sow once in the morning and once again before bedtime to see how much the pelvic bones are separated (see page 65). Be aware that during

Caesarean section. A surgical procedure to deliver unborn pups.

Spotting

If you notice your sow leaving little drops of blood in her bedding at any time during pregnancy, take her to the veterinarian immediately. This "spotting" can indicate a serious problem with the pregnancy.

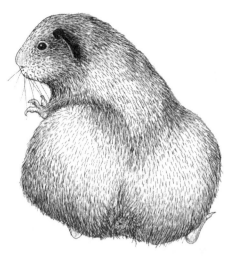

Very pear-shaped sow in late pregnancy.

the first week of pelvic bone separation, the bones may open and close again many times.

Your sow should be touched as little as possible during the last two weeks of her pregnancy. Should you find that you cannot avoid moving your pregnant sow during this time, scoop her up from the rump (do not place hand under belly) and lift her by the shoulders. Carry your pregnant sow close to your body and support her under the rump and around the shoulders. Using the correct method for picking up and transporting your pregnant sow will decrease the chances of problems during transport.

Keep the breeding cage as clean as possible during this time to prevent infections in the sow or the newborn pups after birth.

Remove the Boar Before Birth

A sow will go into her heat cycle within a few hours after she delivers her litter and can therefore become pregnant immediately after giving birth if the boar has

How to carry a pregnant sow.

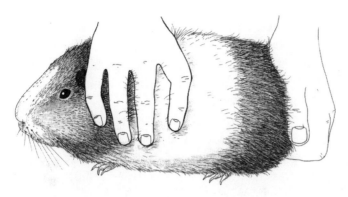

Correct position to hold sow when checking for pelvic bone separation (see below for spot to touch).

not been removed from the breeding cage. This can be very hard on the sow. Also, the boar may trample the newborn pups in his eagerness to breed to the sow.

Labor and Birth

When the time comes for your sow to give birth, she will not make a nest or do anything special in preparation for this event. She will simply pick a spot in her cage, go through labor, and deliver her litter.

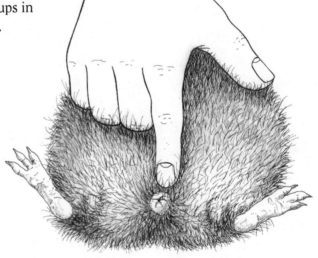

The place to gently touch to determine pelvic bone separation (while in above position).

The process of giving birth is called *labor*. Your sow should not need any help during labor. If you are fortunate enough to be there when this miracle occurs, you will notice that your sow seems to have the hiccups and that she keeps checking her genital area. As a pup comes out of the sow's body, she will quickly tear the membrane sac away from the pup's nose and mouth so the pup can breathe.

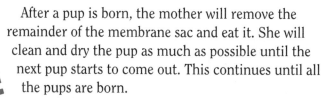

When There's a Problem During Birth

If your sow continues to be in labor — pushing and squealing — for 20 minutes, take her to the veterinarian immediately.

Labor. *The process of giving birth.*

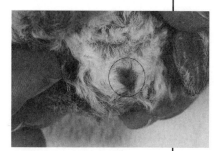

If the pup's genitals are Y-shaped, you have a sow.

If the pup's genitals look like an i, you have a boar.

After a pup is born, the mother will remove the remainder of the membrane sac and eat it. She will clean and dry the pup as much as possible until the next pup starts to come out. This continues until all the pups are born.

While the mother takes care of the newest addition to her family, you may gently open the ears of the pups she is currently ignoring and smooth out the folds. (This is especially good to do with show guinea pigs.) Depending on the size of the litter, the birth process should take from 10 to 30 minutes.

After the Pups Are Born

As the pups are born, the *placenta* or *afterbirth* is also expelled from the mother's body. The placenta is tissue that allows nutrients from the sow's blood to reach the unborn pups and carries waste away. After all the pups are born, the mother usually eats some or all of the placenta. As soon as possible after all the pups have been born, clean up all the mess from the birth, including any remaining placenta.

Sexing Pups

The new pups may be sexed as soon as they are completely dry. A sow's genital area looks like a Y and a boar's genital area looks like an i.

Care of Pups

Newborn pups look like miniature adult guinea pigs. Within hours they will be running around the cage and nibbling at food. For the first 2 to 3 days after they are born, they get most of their food by nursing from their mother.

A mother guinea pig nursing her pup.

If the pups look skinny and hungry after 1 day, you may need to supplement their diet by feeding them with an eyedropper. For the first 5 days, use 1 part dry kitten milk replacer and 2 parts water. Starting on the sixth day, add a little high-protein baby cereal. Keep the mixture thin enough to use with the eyedropper. Do not force the food or milk into the pups. Hold the eyedropper in front of a pup with just one drop of milk or food on the end and let the pup take it on his own.

Guinea pig pups will be eating regular food when they are between 3 and 4 weeks of age. Introduce food supplements — alfalfa, vitamin C sources, treats — as described on pages 28–32. Regular food and water should be available to the pups at all times.

Care of Orphan Pups

Should your sow die giving birth or shortly after, you will need to care for the orphan pups. They will need to be fed by plastic eyedropper every 2 to 3 hours for the first week. Begin with the formula described above.

Placenta. *Tissue that, during pregnancy, carries nutrients to unborn pups and carries waste away.*

When the Sow Needs Your Help

Sometimes a first-time mother doesn't do a good job of removing the membrane, and a pup is in danger of suffocating. If you notice that the membrane still covers a pup's mouth and nose, and the pup doesn't seem to be moving or breathing:

- Make sure your hands are clean.

- Reach into the cage and gently pick up the pup.

- Carefully tear the sac away from the pup's mouth and nose.

- If the pup does not breathe immediately, briskly rub the pup's sides with a soft cloth to stimulate the pup.

- Gently put the pup back into the cage.

Also place a dish of milk sop in the cage twice a day. Be sure to remove the milk sop before it spoils. Regular feed pellets and water (from a water bottle) should be available to pups at all times.

After the first week, you may offer the orphan pups feed pellets soaked in milk. Continue feeding with the eyedropper until the pups are on solid food.

Weaning

Check the sow's teats twice a day to make sure that she is not getting *mastitis* or an infection from a bite by an eager pup. The sow will nurse her litter for about 3 weeks. Somewhere in the third week she will *wean* the pups. Weaning is the gradual decreasing of nursing until the pups are totally off the sow's milk and eating only solid food. Be sure to introduce all the various food supplements (carrots, parsley, broccoli, etc.) to the pups slowly, starting in the third week, so the pups can become accustomed to them. Too many new foods introduced all at once may cause diarrhea. To prevent mastitis, make sure the sow is no longer producing milk before you remove the last pup from the sow's cage.

A guinea pig's diet is usually set during the first months after birth, and the guinea pig may later refuse to eat new foods that it did not receive early in life. That's why it's important to introduce your young guinea pigs to foods that are important sources of vitamin C.

Housing Pups

Between the third and fourth weeks after birth, the boar pups should be separated from the mother and sisters. Brothers may be housed together if you have a

Milk Sop

If your sow has a large litter of four or more, you should offer *milk sop* (bread crumbs soaked in cow's milk) to the pups and mother. This is a good idea because the sow only has two teats for nursing her litter. Do not leave milk sop in the cage for more than one hour because it can spoil.

Weaning. The process by which pups stop nursing and begin to eat solid food.

cage that is large enough.

Sow pups may stay with their mother for a longer time if the cage is large enough.

Place show guinea pigs in individual, separate cages after they are weaned.

Classifying Your Guinea Pig Pups

When the pups are weaned, you need to determine which ones you will keep for future showing or breeding. Then you should determine how the rest of the litter will be sold: as pet stock, show stock, or breeding stock. The A.R.B.A. *Standard of Perfection* will be very useful for making these determinations.

If a boar begins to behave like a breeding boar (cooing, purring, mounting) at an earlier age, he should be removed immediately. This is important because you do not want him mating with his mother or his sisters when he and his sisters are too young.

Identification of Weaned Pups

Your new pups will need identification when they are weaned. Each pup should have a card with the following information placed on its cage: name, ear tag number, sex, breed, variety, color, birth date, sire, and dam. At around 3 months of age, the pups should be tagged or tattooed with their permanent identification number.

Tom	#53	Boar
Peruvian	Broken	Lilac/White/Red
	2-16-94	
Sam #27		Maggie #34

Pup's cage card shows pup's name, ear number, sex, breed, variety, color, birthday, sire, and dam.

An ear tag is a small, thin strip of metal with numbers or letters embossed on it. An ear tag is permanently placed in a guinea pig's left ear using a special plier. A tattoo is permanent ink applied to the skin of the ear with needles. Ear tags and tattoos keep your guinea pigs from being confused with each other and with another breeder's guinea pigs at a show. (See "Managing Your Caviary," page 116.)

At this time, you should write each pup's pedigree if you have not already done so. (See "Managing Your Caviary," page 123.)

Grooming Your Guinea Pig

CHAPTER 6

Why Groom Your Guinea Pig?

Grooming is as important to the health of your guinea pig as proper diet and safe living quarters. Even the cleanest cage will not help a guinea pig through *shedding* as much as a good combing or brushing. When a guinea pig is shedding, it is losing hair so that new hair can grow in its place. Combing, brushing, and, in some cases, bathing are the only ways to really get your guinea pig clean. Grooming helps you find lice or mites sooner than if you wait until these little parasites cause hair loss. You can start treatment earlier for such problems if you spot them during regular grooming sessions.

Grooming is also very important when you show your guinea pig. Everything else being equal, the cleanest, neatest, healthiest, best-presented guinea pig will win over a poorly presented, dirty opponent. Grooming can really make a difference.

Grooming helps a guinea pig look its best by being clean and neat, but it does not change any other aspects of its appearance.

Grooming Is Not Faking

Faking is deliberately changing an animal's appearance in order to deceive a judge or a potential buyer. Darkening toenails with paint or a marker or plucking out spots of foreign colored hair are examples of faking. The consequence of faking is that you will never be allowed to show your guinea pig ever again.

Knowing When to Groom

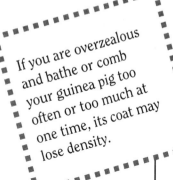

If you are overzealous and bathe or comb your guinea pig too often or too much at one time, its coat may lose density.

You should groom your guinea pig on a regular basis. When and how much you groom your guinea pig depends on the breed and on the individual guinea pig. Long-haired breeds require more grooming than short-haired breeds, and some guinea pigs keep themselves cleaner than others. You'll groom more often when your guinea pig is shedding. As you get to know your guinea pig, you'll be able to judge when it's time to groom.

Toenail Clipping

The toenails of your guinea pig must be kept short to keep them from breaking off and to prevent them from curling under as they grow and poking into the foot-pads. Also, if its nails are too long, your guinea pig might scratch and injure itself or you.

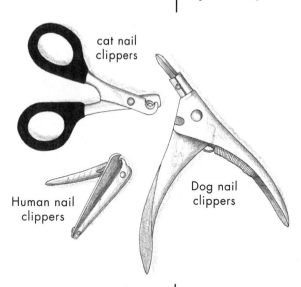

cat nail clippers

Human nail clippers

Dog nail clippers

Nail clippers made for humans, dogs, or cats may be used for trimming your guinea pig's toenails, depending on which you feel the most comfortable using. Have some styptic powder handy and ready to use in case you cut a nail too short.

Hold your guinea pig on its rump or back close against your body or in your lap. Get help the first time you try clipping nails and until you and your guinea pig are comfortable with the procedure.

Before you cut a nail, look very carefully through the nail for the quick. The quick is a bit of flesh inside the nail; it has little blood vessels running through it and appears pink in color. The quick is very easy to see when the guinea pig's nails are white or clear. To find the quick in a dark-colored nail, hold a good, bright light behind it. Do not cut the quick! If you do accidentally cut the quick, place some styptic powder on the nail immediately to stop any bleeding. Give your guinea pig a little rest, then finish clipping the nails.

Getting Ready

Be sure you bathe your guinea pig in a warm draft-free area. You'll need a sink or a dishpan for your guinea pig's bathtub. Use a tearless baby shampoo. If necessary, follow the bath with a good lice and mite shampoo made for cats or birds. (Do not use lice or mite shampoo made for dogs!) If you are bathing long-haired breeds, you will also need a tearless hair conditioner. A multitemperature blow-dryer is useful at bath time, too.

The Bath

Place a towel in the bottom of the sink or dishpan and add 1 to 2 inches of lukewarm water. Place your guinea pig's rump in the water first. Hold the forelegs and chest out of the water at all times. Gently pour water over the shoulders, back, and rump.

Add a little shampoo and work up a good lather.

Work small sections at a time, cleaning the hair from the body outward. On long-haired breeds be very careful not to tangle the hair. When you are satisfied your guinea pig is clean, rinse thoroughly. For long-haired breeds, continue with conditioner. Follow the directions on the conditioner and then rinse twice thoroughly.

Place your guinea pig on a large bath towel. Pull the towel up around

Toe

Quick

Cut line

Nail

Location of quick and cutting lines on guinea pig's toenail

Don't Bathe a Show Teddy or Abyssinian

Never give a bath to a Teddy or an Abyssinian that you plan to use for show! Bathing ruins the texture of the coat on these breeds, making them too soft and less resilient. You'll have to wait many months before the coat is back in show condition. If you find that you must bathe your Teddy or Abyssinian, do not use a conditioner of any type.

> Take care not to get water, shampoo, or conditioner in the guinea pig's eyes, ears, nose, or mouth.

Proper position for guinea pig during a bath:
resting on its rump, your hand keeping
its head out of the water.

your guinea pig and rub gently to get most of the water out of the coat.

Place your guinea pig on another towel to finish drying with a blow-dryer. Use the low-heat setting (not cool, cold, or hot), keep the blow-dryer 5 to 6 inches away, and keep moving it around the coat to keep your guinea pig from getting too hot. When drying long-haired breeds, use a metal wide-tooth comb to separate and comb the hair as you dry.

It's especially important to keep your guinea pig away from drafts after a bath. Make certain your

Using wide-tooth metal comb while
drying long-haired breeds.

guinea pig is completely dry before putting it back into its living quarters. If you do not have a blow-dryer, an aquarium or pet cage is a good and safe place to put your guinea pig until you are sure it is dry. Place a towel on the floor of the aquarium or plastic cage instead of shavings and make sure there is food and water.

Grooming the Teddy

You should have the following items for grooming your Teddy: a metal flea comb, a wide-tooth metal comb, and a slicker brush. Metal combs and brushes will not split or break the hair as plastic combs might.

Place your Teddy on a carpet sample on a table in a draft-free area. Begin grooming with the flea comb. Start at the head and comb toward the rear to thoroughly remove shavings and shedding hair from the coat. Do not worry when this causes the coat to lay down, because you will lift the coat in the next step.

When you have combed the coat clean with the flea comb, replace it with the wide-tooth comb. Begin near the head and comb a small section of the coat toward the head. After this small section is standing up, move a little more toward the rump and comb that section toward the head so it stands up. Continue with this technique until you have combed the entire coat.

Finish the grooming session with the slicker brush. Gently catch the tips of the hair and comb up on the sides and toward the head on the rump and back.

At a show, on the way to the judging table, you should pet your Teddy from rump to head to help make the hair stand up.

Metal flea comb, slicker brush, and metal wide-tooth comb for grooming a Teddy.

Small spray bottle and soft, baby brush for grooming an American breed.

You need to put long-haired breeds in rag curlers as soon as their hair is long enough to do so. Until then you must be very aggressive about keeping the hair untangled and clean.

Grooming the American

While your hands will work quite well for grooming your American, you may want to have the following items available: a small spray bottle of water, a soft, baby hairbrush, and a leather chamois or the foot part of a nylon stocking.

Place your American on a carpet sample on a table in a draft-free area. Rub the coat from the rump to the head with your hands, chamois, or stocking. This will loosen and help remove dirt and shedding hair. Spray the guinea pig's coat with a little water to help shedding hair stick to your hands or the chamois. After you have removed the dirt and shedding hair in this manner, rub the hair from head to rump, using your hands, a chamois or stocking, or a soft, baby hairbrush. This moves the hair back into the correct position and distributes the natural oils in the coat.

Grooming the Peruvian and Silkie

You will need the following to groom your Peruvian or Silkie: wax paper, lightweight paper towel or tissue, small rubber bands, metal wide-tooth comb. The paper towel and wax paper are used to make "rag curlers." The rubber bands are used to hold the rag curlers in place. The paper towel or tissue helps hold the hair in place, and the wax paper helps keep out moisture and dirt. The metal comb will not split or break the hair as a plastic comb might.

First, part the rear sweep of the guinea pig's long hair into two sections and the side sweeps into two or three sections.

To prepare rag curlers, cut wax paper and paper towel into 6 or 8 strips just longer than the guinea pig's hair and three times the width of each section.

Step 1: Side sweep parted to determine length and width of rag curlers.

Step 2: Wrap paper towel around hair.

Step 3: Wrap wax paper around paper towel.

Step 4: Fold rag curler in half a second time.

Fold the wax paper and paper towel into three sections along the length.

Now bathe and dry your long-haired guinea pig if a bath is needed. You don't have to bathe your Silkie or Peruvian every time you put its hair in the rag curlers.

As soon as the hair is dry, part it again into sections. On a Peruvian, remember to carefully part the hair down the middle of the back. Do not put the frontal (head furnishings) of a Peruvian in rag curlers. Do not part the hair in any way on a Silkie. Gently twist a Silkie's mane so it will not part.

Step 5: Long-haired breed in rag curlers held in place with rubber bands.

Wrap each section of hair in a strip of paper towel and then wrap a strip of wax paper around the paper towel. Fold the section in half and then fold it in half again. Place a rubber band around the section to hold everything in place. Wrap each section in this manner.

A Silkie or Peruvian guinea pig used for show must be kept in rag curlers all the time. Remove them every few days and comb the hair enough to make sure there are no tangles, and then replace them. Use a new paper towel and wax paper as needed, but at least every other time. At a show, remove the rag curlers and comb the hair just before you take your guinea pig to the judging table. Do not forget to wrap your guinea pig after it has been judged for the last time.

Grooming the Abyssinian for a Show

You will need the following to groom your Abyssinian: cornmeal and a soft, small toothbrush.

About a week before a show, sprinkle a small amount of cornmeal over your Abyssinian to absorb oil and dirt. Be careful not to get cornmeal in the eyes or ears.

A day or two before the show, place your guinea pig on a carpet sample on a table in a draft-free area. Carefully comb the cornmeal out of your Abyssinian's coat with the soft, small toothbrush. This leaves the coat clean but retains the desired harsh texture. Comb each rosette from the center outward and comb each ridge to stand up.

Marketing Your Guinea Pigs

The pups are weaned and you have determined which you will keep and how the rest may be used: designated pet, show, or breeding. What do you do now? You determine the selling price of each guinea pig and then advertise!

Price

The designation given to each pup (pet, show, breeding) helps determine the selling price. Pets are usually sold for the least amount of money, show guinea pigs for the most money, and breeding stock somewhere in between but closer to the show price than the pet price. This is especially true for sows.

Check the prices of guinea pigs at a local pet store. You will usually be able to sell your pet stock at a price that is slightly lower than that charged by a pet shop because you do not have the same expenses a pet store has.

What do most of the breeders you know charge for various stock? The prices they use will give you a good guideline for pricing your stock.

Advertising

Begin by telling your relatives and friends that you have some guinea pigs to sell. Let them know what breeds, varieties, and sexes you have available as well as what quality (pet, show, breeding) is available, and your price ranges. Some of them may buy a guinea pig from you, or may have a friend who would like to buy one.

Signs

One way to bring customers your way is to place attractive, easy-to-read signs with pictures on bulletin boards at feed stores, grocery stores, and veterinarians' offices. The signs should have your name, address and/

Guinea Pigs For Sale

Abyssinian Juniors Intermediates Seniors

Pets • Show • Breeding
**Red, Red/White, Tortoise Shell & White
$5.00-$25.00**

Pocket Pets Caviary	Pocket Pets Caviary

Business Cards Please Take One
Pocket Pets Caviary
Stanley Donrey • (707) 555-1234

Sign to post in feed store.

or telephone number, and what breeds, varieties, and sexes you have for sale. The signs should also tell what quality guinea pigs are available as well as the price range. A "Guinea Pigs for Sale" sign in your front yard also may bring customers.

Demonstrations

Show your guinea pigs off at day care centers and at schools; such demonstrations may get someone interested in the hobby. Tell about the care and housing of your guinea pigs. Take some of the grooming tools or food supplements to demonstrate to the students.

Business Cards

You might consider using business cards. You might place business cards on bulletin boards at feed stores and grocery stores along with your signs. Business cards are also handy to give to potential buyers at shows.

GUINEA PIGS
FOR
SALE

American & Silkie
Ask for Stanley
(707) 555-1234

Sign for front yard.

Pocket Pets Caviary

American & Silkie
Guinea Pigs

Stanley Donrey
(707) 555-1234

1625 Sommerset Ct.
Los Angeles, California 96123

Business card.

Shows

Use a blackboard or dry board at shows to list the stock you have for sale. Don't forget to check show catalogs for rules about guinea pig sales. Some shows have a designated area where animals are to be sold. Some shows ask for a percent of the sale price in exchange for allowing the sale of animals.

Customer Relations

The best advertising is a satisfied customer. If buyers are happy with the way they are treated during the sale and are also happy with the guinea pigs they buy from you, they will tell their friends. They will also tell their friends if you were rude or if you sold a show animal that was disqualified the first time it was shown. If you treat customers as you would like to be treated, you should have no problems selling your guinea pigs.

Have Pedigrees Ready

Make sure you have pedigrees written for all guinea pigs that you are selling as show or breeding stock. Many buyers will not buy the best guinea pig in the world if the pedigree is not with the animal at the time of sale. They have already learned the hard way not to trust someone who says, "I will mail you the pedigree as soon as I get home."

Answer Customers' Questions

Answer all questions as clearly and as honestly as you can. Answer letters asking about your guinea pigs promptly. Inform potential buyers when stock will be available if you do not have it now. Never ignore potential customers or they will quickly find another seller.

Guinea Pig Health and Quality

Only sell healthy stock and make sure it is designated correctly as pet, show, or breeding. Do not sell a pet-quality guinea pig as a show animal or a show animal without a pedigree as a pet. In all sales, make sure you do not sell a breeding sow that is too old to be a breeder.

Matching Customers and Guinea Pigs

Make sure the buyer understands what he or she is about to buy. Try to determine if this is, in fact, the right breed for this customer. Long-haired breeds may look just like shaggy dogs that fit in the palm of your hand and are "oh so cute," but it takes a lot of the owner's time to keep them looking that way. A very busy or lazy customer may be much happier if he or she is steered toward a breed that requires little or no grooming. You might lose a sale now, but this strategy will pay off in more sales later because this customer will remember who sent him or her to the perfect pet.

Guinea Pig Care Kit

Put together a Guinea Pig Care Kit for your especially important customers. This is for first-time buyers who have never owned a guinea pig before. The kit will help new owners who probably have not yet purchased food for their new pet or who have not yet learned much about guinea pig care.

Place the following in a paper bag or large plastic bag: a zip-seal sandwich bag of guinea pig pellets; a brochure (you can create your own) on guinea pig care; your business card or name, address, and telephone number on a

Prepare a Guinea Pig Care Kit to give to new owners.

piece of paper; and the pedigree of a show or breeding animal. Label the bag "Guinea Pig Care Kit." Add a picture of your breed if you like. (See page {00} for pictures you can copy.)

A Box or Bag for the Trip to a New Home

Most new buyers do not realize that they need a container to carry home their new pet. Many exhibitors at shows do not plan on acquiring a new animal so they do not bring extra carry cages. It may help make a sale if you have a way for the exhibitor to get the guinea pig home in comfort. Have good boxes of the proper size or put two large grocery paper bags together to put the guinea pig in for traveling to its new home. Put shavings, a carrot and/or some parsley and maybe an alfalfa cube in the bag or box for the guinea pig to eat during the trip.

Stand Behind Your Sales

Sometimes things go wrong. Do your best to make your customers happy. Replace or buy back guinea pigs from unhappy customers. The good will may very well bring you more sales.

Guinea Pig Handling and Showmanship

CHAPTER 8

Purpose

In showmanship competition, *you* are being judged, not your guinea pig. Whether you want to compete or not, it is very important to learn showmanship with your guinea pig to the very best of your ability. The benefits of learning showmanship are:

1. You learn to handle your guinea pig safely and confidently.

2. Your guinea pig will become used to being handled so you can examine it closely should a problem arise. It will also become used to being handled in the manner it will be handled by a judge at a show. This makes it easier for a judge to examine your guinea pig and place it properly.

3. You learn to thoroughly examine your guinea pig for signs of illness. This is very important because it enables you to begin necessary treatments as early as possible.

4. You learn to thoroughly examine your guinea pig for quality. This is especially important if you are showing or breeding for show.

5. If you decide to compete in showmanship, every competition helps you improve your skills in handling and examining your guinea pig. When you enter a showmanship competition and your score increases, you are a step closer to having a happier, healthier, better-quality guinea pig. This may eventually make you and your guinea pig big winners on and off the show table.

Preparation

Proper preparation for showmanship helps the routine go smoothly. You should practice your showmanship routine as if you are actually in a competition. This will help you eliminate bad habits from the start.

Choose Carefully

If possible, choose a guinea pig that has a very calm, cooperative attitude and does not make a lot of noise while being handled. Try to use a guinea pig of a size that feels comfortable in your hands. If you have small hands, you will do better with a young, small guinea pig. If you have large hands, you will do better with a good-sized, adult guinea pig.

You can sometimes even use a pet guinea pig that has disqualifications if it meets all of the other important criteria for competition — it is calm, cooperative, quiet, and the proper size. If you use a disqualified animal, you must tell the judge about the disqualifications as you find them during your routine. Please note that in some cases, such as state fairs, the rules may require that you use only a good show animal for showmanship competition.

The chosen guinea pig should also show that it receives the best of care — clean, trimmed toenails and a healthy coat (all of which are taken into consideration during showmanship judging).

Dress Properly

Wear long sleeves every time you handle your guinea pigs to help prevent scratches on your arms; short sleeves are not proper attire when handling guinea pigs. If you have long hair, keep it pulled back out of your face and out of the way of your hands. If you wear a tie, make sure it is tacked to your shirt or tucked inside your shirt. Don't wear dangly jewelry, such as bracelets, necklaces, and earrings. Some judges even require that watches be removed. Do not wear loose knit shirts or blouses because your guinea pig's toenails may get tangled in its threads. Do not wear oversized or bulky shirts or blouses because these may get in the way of movement during the routine.

Practice and Learn

Practice at least twice a day, 3 to 4 days a week in a quiet area that has a table. Set up the table with a carpet sample and move the chairs away before you get your guinea pig. Place your guinea pig in its carry cage 3 or 4 feet from the table.

Be calm and patient with your guinea pig and yourself. Pet and/or talk to your guinea pig to help it relax. Practice will help you learn the best way to be in control of your guinea pig, while still being gentle.

Do not try to learn everything all at once. Learn and practice all the components of showmanship a few at a time. For example, learn and practice the Catch and Carry and the Presentation (see page 89) over several days. Then add the examination of the ears and eyes to what you already know, and so on.

Showmanship Competition Format

Different clubs and organizations have different ways of putting on showmanship competitions. Some clubs require exhibitors to take written tests before they are judged on showmanship. Some clubs have one exhibitor at a time do showmanship for a judge. It is not uncommon, however, for fairs to have 5 to 10 exhibitors doing their showmanship at the same time. No talking is allowed during showmanship competition involving more than one exhibitor at a time, unless the judge specifically asks you a question. Eye contact with the judge is very important, especially when you are doing showmanship along with other exhibitors. Eye contact helps make sure that the judge sees what you are doing. Some judges ask you to trade guinea pigs with another exhibitor. They are looking for confidence and ability to be in control even with an unfamiliar animal.

Classes

Showmanship is usually divided into several different classes. These classes are based on the age and ability of the exhibitors. The number and types of classes depend on the club. Novice class is usually for exhibitors who have never done showmanship. Age does not matter in the novice class, and it is not uncommon for a 10-year-old to take a first place over a 15-year-old. Mini-showmanship is for youth 8-years-old and under. Junior showmanship is usually for 9- to 13-year-olds. Senior showmanship is usually for 14- to 18-year-olds. Some clubs allow the winners of each class to move up to the next class for more competition and experience.

Planning Your Day

On the day of competition, you should determine where you need to be and at what time. Sometimes there is a set order for the competition, and sometimes you determine when you will do showmanship. If your showmanship animal is to be judged in the show and your breed will be judged first thing in the morning, then it is a good idea to plan on doing your showmanship after the judging. If your showmanship guinea pig is going to be judged after lunch, then you should plan on doing your showmanship first thing in the morning. If you plan ahead, you usually do not have to worry about your guinea pig being on the judging table at the same time that you are supposed to be doing showmanship. On occasions when the showmanship schedule does conflict with the guinea pig judging schedule, simply tell the person in charge of showmanship, and he or she will make arrangements for you to do your showmanship at a later time.

At the determined time, you should take your guinea pig, in its carry cage, to the waiting area. Your guinea pig will be much more comfortable waiting in its cage than in your lap, especially if the weather is very warm or cold. Wait quietly and observe how things are organized until it is your turn. Be confident and smile. Learn as much as you can.

Components of Showmanship and Scoring

You will be given a score for each component of the showmanship competition. The highest possible total score is 100.

Catch and Carry, Presentation: 5 points

Open the cage door all the way. Carefully pick up your guinea pig by placing one hand under the rump and the other hand under the chest, with the guinea pig's forelegs between your index finger and middle finger. Your thumb should be curled over the guinea pig's shoulder. Hug your guinea pig close to your body and

The proper way to lift a guinea pig out of a carry cage. Support the rump. Securely hold the front legs between your index and middle fingers, with your thumb curled over the shoulder.

gently turn it so its nose is toward your elbow. Close and latch the cage door. Carry your guinea pig to the table and gently place it on the carpet with the left side toward the judge. Pose your guinea pig. Introduce yourself and your guinea pig: "My name is _____. I am in _____ (4-H Club or FFA). This is _____, my American White Senior Sow."

The judge will score you on how securely and gently you handle your guinea pig, how well you control your guinea pig, and on left-side presentation.

Show the Guinea Pig: 60 points total

You will be scored on how gentle and thorough your examination is and how well you control your guinea pig.

Examine the ears and eyes: 6 points each, or 12 points total.

Begin by examining the left ear. As you examine the left ear, tell and show the judge the ear tag number. Explain to the judge that you are looking for cuts, rips, signs of ear mites and lice, as well as for foreign-colored hair and skin. You are also checking the shape, size, and position of the ear. Tell the judge your findings — for example, no cuts, no foreign hair, etc. Now examine the left eye. Explain to the judge that you are looking for signs of infection (discharge), signs of blindness (cloudy), correct color, and boldness in appearance (large, prominent). Lift the chin slightly and explain that you are looking for pea eye. To examine the right ear and eye, gently lift your guinea pig, carefully supporting the rump and chest so that your guinea pig does not dangle in the air, and turn it so the right side is facing the judge. Examine the right ear as you did the left. Be sure to mention it if your guinea pig is registered and if it is, show the tag. Examine the right eye as you examined the left.

Examine the nose and teeth: 6 points.

Carefully lift your guinea pig and place it on its back so that it is resting comfortably on the table. (This is when your practice can really pay off. It takes time for you to learn this technique and time for your guinea pig to learn to trust you when it is placed in this vulnerable position.) While restraining the guinea pig firmly and gently, examine and show the nostrils to the judge. Explain that you are looking for signs of cold (discharge). Tell the judge your findings (no discharge). Gently move your guinea pig's mouth to expose the teeth. Explain to the judge that you are looking for malocclusion. Tell the judge your findings (no malocclusion, or trimmed teeth due to malocclusion).

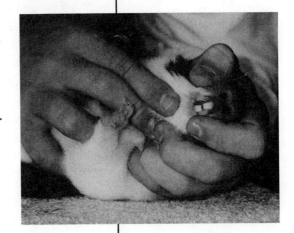

Show the guinea pig's teeth to look for malocclusion.

Examine the front legs: 6 points.

While your guinea pig is still on its back, gently stretch out the front legs and feel along the bones for straight-

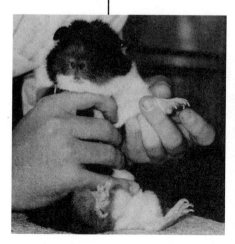
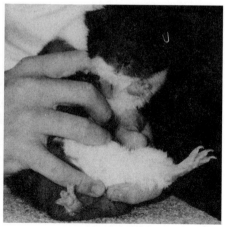

Show front feet and toenails,
checking footpads.

Show hind legs.

ness and signs of old breaks. (The bone may have a bulge somewhere, or it may feel crooked due to not healing properly.) Explain to the judge that you are checking the straightness of the front legs and tell your findings (for example, straight, signs of old break). At this time you should also examine the feet, toes, and toenails. Explain to the judge that you are looking for missing toes and toenails as well as extra toes, and that you are checking the footpads for injury and for color. You are also checking for correct color of toenails and to determine whether the nails need trimming. Tell the judge your findings (no extra toes, no missing toenails, correct color, etc).

Examine the hind legs: 6 points.

While your guinea pig is still on its back, gently stretch out the hind legs and examine them as you did the front legs.

Examine the sex: 6 points.

While your guinea pig is still on its back, examine and show the genital area to the judge. If you are using a sow, you should also examine and show the teats to the judge. Explain to the judge that you are checking the sex of your guinea pig, looking for anal impaction, looking for discharge that may mean infection, and for a sow, checking the number and condition of the teats. Also check for abscesses and hernias on the chin, neck, chest, and abdomen. Tell the judge your findings (sow or boar, no impaction or discharge, no abscesses or hernias, etc.).

Show the guinea pig's sex.

Show the front view: 6 points.

Carefully return your guinea pig to its feet. Position your guinea pig so the head faces the judge at a slight angle to the right and pose it correctly. Place the rear feet directly in line with the hip bone above. Place the front feet directly under the shoulders. Do not stretch out or bunch up the guinea pig. To position the head in a natural position, gently touch the end of the guinea pig's nose. Explain to the judge that you are checking for overall balance and proportions. Tell the judge your findings (well balanced, small head, etc.).

Show the right side view: 6 points.

Carefully turn your guinea pig so the right side is facing the judge and pose it correctly. Explain to the judge that you are checking overall balance. Tell the judge your findings (well balanced, ears too high, etc.).

Show the rear view: 6 points.

Carefully turn your guinea pig so the rump is facing the judge at a slight angle and pose it correctly. Explain to the judge that you are checking width and proportion. Tell the judge your findings (narrow shoulders, etc.).

Show the left side view (scores for right and left sides are combined).

Gently turn your cavy so the left side is facing the judge. Do the same as for the right side, described above.

Show the cleanliness of the fur: 6 points.

Gently rub the hair on the back and sides from rump to head. Explain to the judge that you are checking the cleanliness of the hair, the density, texture, color, and color depth. You are also looking for mites, lice, growth pattern, and foreign color hair. At this time, you should also gently feel the chin, chest, abdomen, and back for abscesses and hernias. Tell the judge your findings (no angle wings, all rosettes in good alignment, ridges straight, good depth of color, no foreign hair, no mites or lice, etc.).

Appearance, Actions, Knowledge: 30 points total

You will be judged on your appearance and your guinea pig's appearance, your actions, and your knowledge. A good appearance shows that you are serious about your hobby and the way you care for your guinea pig. Your actions show how comfortable you are with your animal and whether you really know what you are doing. Your guinea pig's reactions show how comfortable it is when you handle it. Knowledge is important because the more you know, the better care your guinea pig receives. Questions can be about feeding, diseases and conditions, housing, breeding, different breeds or varieties, history, or anything about guinea pigs.

How you act when your guinea pig misbehaves tells a judge quite a lot. It is important to know the difference between firm and rough.

Appearance: 10 points.

You must be neat, clean, and dressed properly: long sleeves, tie tacked or tucked into shirt, hair pulled out of the way, no dangling jewelry, and no oversized or bulky, loose knit shirts. Your nails should be trimmed.

Actions: 10 points.

You should examine everything about your guinea pig in a calm, confident manner. Smile and relax. Be as gentle as possible with your guinea pig. Have your eyes on the judge as much as possible so that your attention is focused on what you are doing and you are sure the judge is seeing what needs to be seen.

Knowledge: 10 points.

You should be prepared to answer questions about breeds, varieties, management, illness, faults, eliminations, and disqualifications. The questions will most likely come from the A.R.B.A. *Standard of Perfection* and/or the A.R.B.A. Guide Book.

Catch and Carry, Return Guinea Pig to Cage: 5 points.

When the judge is finished judging your routine, you will be instructed to return your guinea pig to its cage. Carefully lift your guinea pig and hug it close to your chest. Carry your guinea pig back to its cage and open the cage door. Place your guinea pig in the cage rump first and then close the door and latch it. You may now leave the area, or you may stay to observe other exhibitors. If you remain, you should be quiet and unobtrusive.

Place guinea pig in a carry cage, rump first.

Cavy Showmanship Judging Form

You can use this example of a Cavy Showmanship Judging Form to practice showmanship with your parents or friends.

Name _____

4-H _____ FFA_____

Junior _____ Senior _____

CAVY SHOWMANSHIP

Carry the cavy from cage: 5 points .... _____

Show the cavy: 60 points total

1. Show the ears: 6 points .... _____
2. Show the eyes: 6 points .... _____
3. Show the teeth and nose: 6 points .... _____
4. Show the front legs: 6 points .... _____
5. Show the hind legs: 6 points .... _____
6. Show the sex: 6 points .... _____
7. Show the front view: 6 points .... _____
8. Show the rear view: 6 points .... _____
9. Show the side view: 6 points .... _____
10. Show cleanliness of fur: 6 points .... _____

Appearance, Actions, and Knowledge: 30 points total

1. Appearance: 10 points .... _____
2. Actions: 10 points .... _____
3. Knowledge: 10 points .... _____

Catch and Carry, Return Guinea Pig to Cage: 5 points .... _____

TOTAL _____

Comments:_____

_____

_____

_____

_____

Cavy showmanship judging form.

Showing Your Guinea Pigs

CHAPTER

Showing Pros and Cons

Showing your guinea pigs can be fun and educational. Going to shows puts you, as well as your guinea pigs, in front of many people. Shows can be a good place to advertise and sell your stock.

The down-side of going to shows is that they take a lot of time, usually a whole day, and may be stressful for your guinea pigs. Showing your guinea pigs costs money — entry fees, travel, meals. The expenses may be lowered, however, if you pack a lunch or go with friends. Also, taking only animals that are likely to place (get an award) keeps entry fees down.

Show Etiquette

Before you start showing your guinea pigs, you need to know a little show etiquette.

- Only take healthy animals to a show.

- Arrive at the show early, about a half hour to an hour, so you can set up and be ready to go when the judging begins. No one should have to wait for you when it is time for your animals to be judged.

- Tell the show secretary if you left any animals at home that you entered in the show; these are called no shows or scratches. This keeps people from needlessly looking for an animal to be judged.

- Do not try to let the judge know which animals are yours. Some people think a judge might place an animal differently if he or she knows to whom it belongs.

- Get your animals to the judging table promptly when called. Remove them as soon as the judge says they can be removed from the judging table.

- If you have questions, try to wait until the judge finishes judging the current class. The judge may find a good example in the next class that will help answer your question.

- Be a good winner and a good loser. No one likes an exhibitor who pouts when he or she loses or who brags when he or she wins. Be sure to congratulate the winners. Be gracious if you are the winner. Do not be upset with the judge or comment in any way about his or her judging ability.

- Never say anything bad about another exhibitor or breeder. Things said have a way of coming back to haunt you. If someone asks you about a breeder, it is better to steer them to someone else than tell them a particular breeder is "no good."

Show Classes

A class is a division of competition based on the age and/or weight and sex of the guinea pigs. Cavies are shown as juniors, intermediates, or seniors.

- Juniors must be under 4 months of age. They must weigh more than 12 ounces but not more than 22 ounces.

- Intermediates are over 4 months of age and under 6 months of age. They weigh over 22 ounces up to a maximum of 32 ounces.

- Seniors are over 6 months of age and weigh over 32 ounces.

If your guinea pig is a junior by age (under 4 months) but weighs over 22 ounces, it should be entered in the Intermediate class. If your guinea pig is intermediate by age (between 4 and 6 months of age) but weighs over 32 ounces, it should be entered in the Senior class.

Entering a Show

Cavy shows are held locally, countywide, statewide, and nationwide. They are sponsored by 4-H clubs, local clubs, state clubs, specialty clubs, and by the American Rabbit Breeders Association, Inc. (A.R.B.A.). 4-H may be a good place to start finding out about where and when there may be cavy shows. The A.R.B.A. can provide a list of shows it sanctions (shows that follow A.R.B.A. rules) for you to attend (see "Helpful Sources," page 137 for address).

Show Catalog

Write to the show secretary for a show catalog. This is a book that gives all the information you will need about the show:

- Where and when the show will be held.

- Whether the show is sanctioned by the A.R.B.A. and/or specialty club under A.R.B.A.

- The entry fee (how much each animal will cost to enter the show).

When Your Guinea Pig Doesn't Meet Weight Requirements

- If your guinea pig is a senior by age (over 6 months of age) but weighs less than the required minimum of 32 ounces, it should not be shown.

- If your guinea pig is intermediate by age (between 4 and 6 months of age) but weighs less than 22 ounces, it should not be shown.

- The deadline for the entries (usually something like "Must Be Postmarked No Later Than Midnight, January 10, 1994").

- How long the animals will be kept at the show. (Sometimes fairs keep animals for the entire run of the fair even though they will only be judged on one of those days.)

- Whether this is a carry-on show (you provide the carry cage) or a cooped show (they provide the cage for the show).

- Any special rules you need to know (when the animals will be released after a show, sale rules).

Entry Form

To enter a show you must fill out an entry form with the following information about each guinea pig:

- The ear tag number, which keeps your animal from becoming confused with another.

- The breed of the animal. Your guinea pig will only be judged against other guinea pigs of the same breed, except when being judged for Best in Show.

- The variety of the animal. Your guinea pig will only be judged against other guinea pigs of the same variety, except when being judged for Best of Breed or Best in Show.

- The sex of the animal. Your guinea pig will only be judged against other guinea pigs of the same sex, except when being judged for Best of Variety, Best of Breed, or Best in Show.

- The class of the animal. Your guinea pig will only be judged against other guinea pigs in the same class, except when being judged for Best of Variety, Best of Breed, or Best in Show.

Cavy Show Entry and Report

Entry #: _____ Date of Show: September 10, 1994

Exhibitor/Owner: ___Wanda L. Curran___ Today's Date: September 7, 1994

_____PO Box 001_____ Caviary Name: Curran's Fur Fang & Feather Farm

_____Homeville, CA 00001_____ Phone #: 009-555-1234

ARBA # Open: __Currwa00__ Youth: _____ Specialty Club #s: ACBA 94-110 GSCA 32SS

State Assn. # Open: _____ Youth: _____ Ribbons: ❏ Yes   ❏ No

Coop	Breed & Variety	Ear Number	Sex/Class	Entry Fee	For Secretary's Use Only				
					# in Class	Place	Points	Cash	Specials
	American Cream	48	SOW - Int.						
	American Cream	654	SOW - Int.						
	American White	655	BOAR - Int.						

Total Entry [_____]   Total Cash [_____]

Display Awards:

1. _____ Sponsoring Club: _____

2. _____ Show Location: _____

3. _____ Show Secretary: _____

Total Points: _____

This show entry form printed by The Cavy Register Program Evans Software Service

Cavy show entry form.

- The entry fee. The entry fee must be paid for *each* guinea pig that you wish to enter in the show.

- Your name.

- Your address.

- Your telephone number. If the show secretary discovers that you left some information off of your entry, or if your hand writing is illegible, he or she will call you on the telephone collect to get the information.

Some shows want you to enter using their own special form. Some shows allow you to enter using a blank sheet of paper, provided all the required information is on it. Some clubs have more than one show on the same date, and you will need a separate entry form for each show that you wish to enter. Make sure that you designate on each form which show you are entering. Clubs usually allow you to photocopy entry forms so you will have one for each show. If you are entering more than one show, do not forget to send the entry fees for each show.

Be sure to write legibly so everything can be read without trouble. Use capital letters if the ear tag number includes any letters. Be very careful how numbers are written. It's important to make sure that the number 5 is not confused with S, and Z is not confused with the number 2, and so on.

Preparing for a Show

Examine Your Guinea Pigs

Handle all the guinea pigs that you have entered in the show and check them for health, eliminations, and disqualifications. Take only healthy guinea pigs to shows. If you take a sick animal to a show and it causes another exhibitor's animal to become ill, you will be considered a bad breeder.

Groom

Groom your guinea pigs so they will look their best for judging. (See "Grooming Your Guinea Pig," page 71.)

Ear Tags

Make sure that all your guinea pigs are ear tagged well in advance of the show. (See "Managing Your Caviary," page 116.)

Prepare Carry Cages and Other Equipment

Make sure that you have proper, watertight carry cages to take your guinea pigs to the show. Have a towel or sheet to place over the carry cage if the cage will be near a window and exposed to the sun; a towel or sheet will help keep your guinea pigs from getting too warm. Do not put your guinea pigs in the trunk of your car.

Prepare Grooming Equipment

Pack all necessary grooming equipment. If you will be showing long-haired breeds, pack grooming/show boards (see page 26).

Prepare Food

Prepare the vegetables that you will use for your guinea pigs while in transit to and from the show.

Make Travel Arrangements

Know what your travel arrangements are well in advance of the show.

Do not mail your show entry late and miss the deadline. Send the total entry fee with the entry form. Use a check or money order for entry fees. *Never, never* send cash. Make checks out to the club sponsoring the show, not to the show secretary.

At the Show

Check-In

When you arrive at the show area, check with the show secretary to see if there is a special place, called a coop area, where you are to put your guinea pigs and supplies and/or pick up a checklist or coop cards for all your entries to make sure they were recorded correctly. Coop cards are placed on your carry cages to help quickly identify the guinea pigs in the cages. At this

Sierra Foothill RCBA Cavy Show B

Exhibitor No. 53, Curran, Wanda L.
Number Entered 3

If there are any problems with your entry as shown below please see the show secretary. No corrections or changes can be made at the judging table or after the judging.

In Fur entry column, B indicates the animal is entered in breed fur, C indicates the animal is entered in commercial normal fur, and BC indicates the animal is entered in both.

A question mark (?) in any column indicates the correct information is not known.

Ear #	Coop #	Breed	Color	Class	Sex	Fur
48		American	Cream	Int.	Sow	
654		American	Cream	Int.	Sow	
655		American	White	Int.	Boar	

A checklist is a form listing the guinea pigs you've entered in the show.

```
┌─────────────────────────────────────────┐
│  Entry No.: 53    Ear No.: 48             │
│  American – Variety: Cream                │
│  Class: Int.    Sex: Sow                  │
│  Owner: Wanda L. Curran                   │
│  Adress: PO Box 001                       │
│  City/State: Homeville, CA 00001          │
│  GOLDEN STATE CAVY BREEDERS ASS'N         │
└─────────────────────────────────────────┘
```

Coop cards identify individual guinea pigs at a show.

time, you should make changes if you find any errors on your entry. Let the show secretary know if you have any no-shows.

You will be given an exhibitor number to use during the show. The exhibitor number is used in place of your name to keep you from being identified as the owner of a particular animal. If there is a question about your entry or animals, you will be called by your exhibitor number. For example, "Will exhibitor 25 bring ear number 63, white, American, Senior boar to the judging table."

Get Your Guinea Pigs Settled

Get your guinea pigs settled and comfortable in the coop area. Put water bottles on carry cages and add feed if needed. Place each coop card on its appropriate cage. Cover your guinea pigs' cages with a towel, sheet, or blanket if it is cold or drafty in your coop area.

Find the Judging Table

Find out where your guinea pigs will be judged so you will be able to get your animals to the table quickly at the appropriate time.

Listen for Your Breed and Class to Be Called

Listen carefully for your breed and class to be called to the judging table. Take your animals to the table as soon as they are called. Some shows have carriers — people whose job is to find animals in the coop area, take them to the judging table, and then return them to their cages after judging. Even if there are carriers, it is still your responsibility to be certain that your animals get to and from the judging table.

The Judging Process

When your class is called, take your guinea pig to the judging table and give it to the *ramrod*. The ramrod is the person who checks the ear numbers to make sure all the animals in a class are on the table and then places them in a judging coop. A judging coop is where an animal stays during judging. Once your animals are on the judging table, stand nearby and watch and

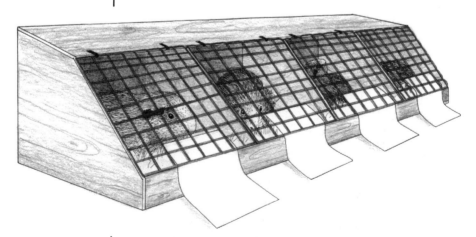

A judging coop holds guinea pigs on the judging table during judging.

The judge examines
a guinea pig as
owners watch.

listen. You can learn quite a lot of information about guinea pigs in general and about your breed by watching and listening to all the judging.

The judge begins judging a class by first checking for eliminations and disqualifications. Any animals found with eliminations or disqualifications are given their comments and removed from the table. The judge then begins to place the remaining guinea pigs from the last or bottom of the class to the first or top of the class. He or she tells the clerk (the person who writes the judge's comments about an animal) all the good points about the guinea pigs and all the faults of the guinea pigs.

The judge determines place number and any special awards an animal will receive (Best of Variety, Best Opposite of Breed, etc.). Guinea pigs that receive a first place award are the winners of their class and usually stay on the table to see if they will move higher on the award scale. (See "Show Awards," below.)

When the judge determines that your guinea pigs can leave the judging table, remove them at once. If you delay removing your guinea pigs, it may delay judging of the next class if there aren't enough judging coops available. You should also see if you are to pick up your comment cards at this time or how you will get your comment cards before you leave the show.

Show Awards

At a show, guinea pigs of the same breed are judged in groups based on age, sex, and variety. The first-place winners in each category within a breed are then judged against each other to determine the best guinea pig of that breed. Finally, all the best guinea pigs from all the breeds (winners of Best of Breed) are judged against each other to find the best of all the guinea pigs at the show, which is named the Best in Show. This is the highest award a guinea pig can receive at a show.

After your guinea pigs have been judged, check your comment cards to see if you have won any awards. Awards begin with simple place ribbons (usually first through third or fifth). The next awards are for Best of Variety and Best Opposite Sex of Variety followed by Best of Breed and Best Opposite Sex of Breed. These awards may be rosettes or trophies. Guinea pigs are also awarded Best Junior, Intermediate, and Senior of Variety and Breed. The awards may be small ribbons or certificates. Some clubs only give ribbons, rosettes, and trophies if there are 10 or more entries in a class, variety, or breed or if someone sponsors a particular award.

When you present your comment cards to the person in charge of awards, any certificates, ribbons, rosettes, or trophies that your guinea pigs may have won will be given to you. Write the ear number, name of the guinea pig, show, and date on each award so you will always know which award belongs with which guinea pig. Remember to send thank you cards or notes to sponsors of any special awards you may have received.

Show trophy.

Sequence of Judging

For each variety within a breed, winners are chosen for:

- Best Junior Boar of Variety
- Best Junior Sow of Variety
- Best Junior of Variety
- Best Intermediate Boar of Variety
- Best Intermediate Sow of Variety
- Best Intermediate of Variety
- Best Senior Boar of Variety
- Best Senior Sow of Variety
- Best Senior of Variety

The Best Junior, Intermediate, and Senior boars and sows of Variety are judged against each other to determine:

- Best of Variety
- Best Opposite Sex of Variety

The Best of Variety and Best Opposite Sex of Variety for all varieties are judged against each other to determine:

- Best of Breed
- Best Opposite Sex of Breed

Finally, the Best of Breed for all breeds (American, American Satin, Abyssinian, Abyssinian Satin, Peruvian, Peruvian Satin, Silkie, Silkie Satin, Teddy, Teddy Satin, and White Crested) are judged against each other to determine:

- Best in Show
- Best Reserve in Show

Legs

A very special award that your guinea pigs can receive is a *leg*. A leg is a special certificate given at A.R.B.A.-sanctioned shows. In order to be awarded a leg, there must be a minimum of three breeders (exhibitors) and a minimum of five guinea pigs in the class, variety, or breed. When your guinea pig is awarded three legs, it is eligible for a Grand Champion Certificate. A Grand Champion Certificate is a very big achievement and increases the value of your guinea pigs for sale and breeding.

Certificate
No. J3135

Date APRIL 15, 1994

Bloomington, Illinois

Grand Champion

of the

American Rabbit Breeders Association, Inc.

This is to certify that the

TEDDY

known as

DOMINO

with registration number B95
and owned by **LEX MILLER** of Marysville, California

has been awarded the status of Grand Champion in recognition of its superior quality, having demonstrated excellence in competition according to the standards of the American Rabbit Breeders Association, Inc. Issuance of this certificate has been recorded in the Registry of Grand Champions.

Glen C. Carr

Secretary

A Grand Champion Certificate recognizes a guinea pig's quality and success in competition.

After the Show

When you arrive home after a long, tiring day at the show, you must take care of your guinea pigs. Carefully check each animal as you place it in its cage. Be sure that there is food and water for the night. Check to see if there are daily chores that still must be done. Some chores cannot wait until tomorrow no matter how late it is and how tired you are.

Place all your comment cards in a safe place so you can study them later. Do not make decisions about your stock from one judge's opinion. Judges have good

Sierra Foothill RCBA Cavy Show B

Gridley, California 09/10/94

Exhibitor No. 53
Curran, Wanda L.
PO Box 001
Homeville, CA 00001

Show Secretary
Wanda L. Curran
PO Box 001
Homeville, CA 00001
(009) 500-4001

American

Coop	Ear	Color	Class–Sex	# In Class	Place	Pts.	Leg
	48	Cream	Int. Sow	5	1	30	Yes
	58	Cream	Int. Sow	5	Elim.	0	
	655	White	Int. Boar	2	2	8	

Judge: Kristy Cavallo   #643, Total Points 38

Thanks for helping make the show a succcess! See you in April!

You should receive a show report within
30 days after a show.

days and bad days. One judge may put the animal in the pet or near-pet category, but three other judges may make that same animal a grand champion.

As you head off to bed, you can smile and reflect on the day and what you have learned. Win or lose, it was a good day after all.

You should receive a show report in the mail, along with any legs your guinea pigs have won, in 30 days or less after the show. If you are positive that you have legs coming, and over 30 days have passed and you haven't received them, you should contact the show secretary. Duplicate legs can be issued to you if the originals were lost in the mail.

Winners show off their ribbons and trophies...and a rabbit one participant won in a raffle at the show!

Managing Your Caviary

Managing your caviary means controlling what happens in your caviary. The success of your caviary depends on how well you organize all the chores that need to be done and then carry through with these chores.

Daily Chores

Feeding and Watering

Guinea pigs become set in their ways. Changes can be stressful for them. They should be fed and watered at the same time each day to reduce stress. Rinse water bottles and sipper tubes thoroughly each time you refill them. Dump dust and fines out of feeders.

Observing Your Guinea Pigs

Feeding time is a good time to observe your guinea pigs. Look for changes in behavior, injuries, or signs of illness.

Unscheduled Cleaning or Repairs

Clean up spilled feed, etc., at the time it is spilled. If a light needs to be replaced, replace it as soon as you

Chore Categories

- Daily chores.
- Weekly chores.
- Monthly chores.
- Ear tagging.
- Ear tattooing.
- Record-keeping.

notice it. Cleaning up messes when they happen and making repairs as soon as you spot the need makes your job easier over time.

Handle Your Guinea Pigs

If you have several guinea pigs, you should handle a few of them each day. This gives you a chance to examine them closely and keeps them used to being handled. Handling your guinea pigs is a very good way to help your guinea pigs tolerate stress.

Weekly Chores

Clean Trays

This is actually a job you must do 2 or 3 times a week. If you smell ammonia in your caviary, you have waited too long to clean your cages. Ammonia is very dangerous for your guinea pigs and can cause severe respiratory problems. Once a week, wash trays in soapy water. (See "Guinea Pig Housing and Equipment," page 26.)

Clean Feeders and Drinking Bottles

Cleaning feeders and drinking bottles weekly is vital to your guinea pigs' health. (See "Guinea Pig Housing and Equipment," page 26.)

Examine Guinea Pigs

Once a week, thoroughly examine all of your guinea pigs for any health problems.

Check Supplies

Do you have enough pellets for the weekend? How soon will you need to buy new pellets? Check the date on the pellets. Are they over 90 days old?

Make Repairs

Do you see any equipment or cages that need repair?
Do any trays need to be replaced?

Observe Breeding Sows

Prepare for coming events. How soon will a sow *kindle?*
Is there separation of the pelvic bones? Should the boar
be removed? How are the new mother and litter doing?
Is it time to remove boar pups from the sow and
sisters?

Kindle. *Give birth.*

Monthly Chores

Trim Toenails

Once a month, check each guinea pig's toenails and
trim them properly. (See "Grooming Your Guinea
Pigs," page 72.)

Check Ventilation and Lighting

Are the fans working properly? Do they need oil? Do
you need a larger or more powerful fan because you
have added more animals to your caviary? Is there
enough light for all the guinea pigs?

Sterilize All Equipment and Cages

Washing equipment and trays once a week helps keep
germ populations under control for a while. If your
equipment and cages, however, are not sterilized once
a month, the germs have a better chance of getting out
of control. (See "Guinea Pig Housing and Equipment,"
page 26.)

Ear Tagging

Assigning Identification Numbers

Before you write a pedigree for a pup, you must assign it an ear tag number to be used for identification purposes. The number assigned is usually on the first available ear tag from a package of tags. The ear tag must be placed in the left ear. The right ear is used for registration.

Helpful Hint

A little bit of bright red nail polish brushed over the numbers on the tag and then wiped off carefully will leave enough polish in the numbers to make them easier to read.

An ear tag is placed in the left ear.

A registration tag is placed in the right ear.

Order ear tags through the mail. (See "Helpful Sources," pages 137–138.) They are usually available in minimum quantities of 100. You may order the numbers you need from 1 to 100 or 101 to 200 and so on. The cost is around $16.00 to $20.00. You may order special, personalized ear tags that begin with a letter followed by numbers or that consist only of letters, at a bit higher cost. A lot of clubs and show secretaries make ear tags available for a small fee.

Ear Tag Pliers

You need ear tag pliers to place the ear tag in the ear. You can order them through the mail. Work the pliers open and closed until they do not stick in any position. It is very important that the pliers open quickly after the tag is applied to avoid ripping the guinea pig's ear. Notice that the bottom of the pliers is straight and the top of the pliers has a notch. The notch allows the pointed part of the tag to go through the hole in the top of the tag before it bends to lock the tag in place. It is a good idea to gently close the tag with your fingers to make sure the pointed end goes through the hole correctly. If the hole and pointed end do not line up properly, you must align them before you use the tag. Once you are sure the hole in the top of the tag aligns with the pointed end, you can place the tag in the pliers.

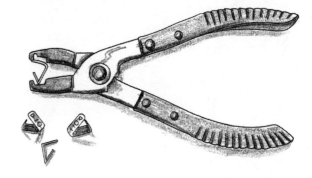

Ear tag pliers and ear tags.

Placement of the Ear Tag

The correct position for the ear tag is in the top of the ear, where the ear is thicker, and at the front of the ear. You must be careful not to fold the ear in the ear tag

Correct position for ear tag.

Ear folded in ear tag.

Ear tag with a little space to allow for growth on pup.

when you tag your guinea pigs. If the ear tag is placed too low in the ear, it is easier for the guinea pig to rip it out when scratching its ear. If you are placing the ear tag in a growing pup, make sure that you leave room for growth.

Ear Tagging Procedure

You will need help from a friend to hold the guinea pig still when you first begin placing ear tags in the ears of your guinea pigs. Later, as you gain experience, you should be able to place ear tags alone.

The ear tagging of a guinea pig is very similar to humans having their ears pierced. If done correctly, it happens very quickly and is over almost before the guinea pig notices. The guinea pig may jump with surprise and may give a quick squeek or two, much the same as humans would say "Ouch!," but it will settle down very quickly. The pliers press the pointed part of the ear tag through the guinea pig's ear, then through the hole in the ear tag. Once the pointed part of the ear tag is through the hole, it hits the notch in the top of the pliers and bends over the hole. Once bent, it is extremely difficult to unbend the pointed part of the ear tag to remove the ear tag.

1. Gather all tagging supplies — ear tag pliers, ear tag(s), styptic powder, guinea pig(s).

2. Check the ear tag number to be certain that you have the correct tag for that guinea pig. It is too difficult and dangerous to remove an ear tag once in place.

3. Check the alignment of point and hole of ear tag — pinch the ear tag closed between your thumb and index finger to check.

4. Have a friend hold the guinea pig close to her body with the body of the guinea pig in her left hand and the head in her right hand. Make sure

the left ear is exposed and easy to get to with the pliers and ear tag.

5. Place the tag in the pliers, making sure the hole is near the notch in the top.

6. Make sure that there are no folds or wrinkles in the front of the ear, near the head.

7. Hold the ear, position the pliers.

8. Squeeze the pliers hard, then quickly release your grip on the pliers so they open quickly to release the ear tag.

9. If there is a little bleeding, sprinkle styptic powder on the area and allow it to stop bleeding. Leave the ear alone and it will heal in a few days. (Bleeding occurs very rarely.)

10. Place the guinea pig back in its cage and give it a small treat.

11. Check the ear tag site once a day for 2 or 3 days for infection. (I have never had a single infection from ear tagging, but I believe this is a good practice.)

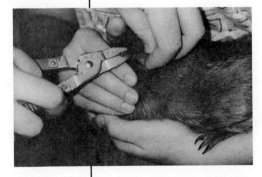

A friend can hold the guinea pig while you place the ear tag.

Ear Tattooing

Ear tattooing, like ear tagging, is much the same as ear piercing for humans. You can use a single-needle tattoo needle (it really has three needles, one of which is longer than the other two) or tattoo pliers with digits set into them to make combinations of numbers or letters. Ear tattooing for guinea pigs is not as popular in this country as it is in England and Europe because the procedure is a bit more complicated than ear tagging.

Tattoo pliers with letter and number and ink

Tattooing supplies may be purchased through the mail or at feed stores. (See "Helpful Sources," pages 137–138.) Have a friend help you tattoo your guinea pigs.

Ear Tattooing Procedure with Tattooing Pliers

1. Gather all tattooing supplies — tattooing pliers, letters and/or numbers, and blanks, alcohol, clean cloth, cotton swabs, tattoo ink, petroleum jelly, clean scrap paper, guinea pig(s).

2. Wipe the top of the guinea pig's left ear with alcohol to remove any dirt and oils.

3. Place the correct numbers and/or letters in the tattoo pliers. Because a guinea pig's ears are so small, only two or three numbers are usually used. Place the blanks in the pliers to help hold the numbers in place. Be sure that the numbers fit tightly in place.

4. Check that the numbers are correct by pressing the needles through a piece of scrap paper.

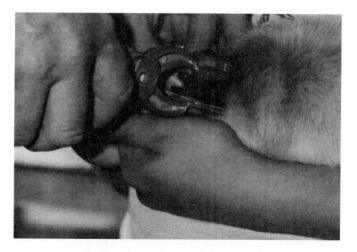

One person should hold the guinea pig while the other puts the tattoo pliers in position.

5. Have your friend hold the guinea pig close to his body with the body of the guinea pig in his left hand and the head in his right hand. Make sure that the guinea pig's left ear is exposed and easy to reach with the tattoo pliers.

6. Make sure that there are no folds or wrinkles in the ear.

7. Place the tattoo pliers so the needles will go through the ear from the top.

8. Squeeze the tattoo pliers hard, then release them quickly so the needles come out of the ear quickly.

9. Place a little tattoo ink on a cotton swab and rub the ink into the holes in the ear. Add ink as needed. (Green tattoo ink works reasonably well in dark-colored ears.) The ink will stop any bleeding caused from the needles.

10. Wipe off any excess ink and rub a little petroleum jelly over the holes to protect the ink until the holes heal with the ink inside.

11. Return the guinea pig to its cage and give it a small treat.

12. Check for infection of the ear once a day for 2 or 3 days.

Ear Tattooing with Single Needle

1. Gather tattooing supplies — single needle, fine-tip felt pen, tattoo ink, small, rectangular rubber eraser, small lid or container for holding a small amount of ink, alcohol, clean cloth, guinea pig(s).

2. Clean top of left ear with alcohol on the clean cloth.

3. Shake the ink well, then pour a small amount into a small container.

4. Have your friend hold the guinea pig close to her body with the body of the guinea pig in her left hand and the head in her right hand. Make sure the left ear is exposed and easy to reach for tattooing.

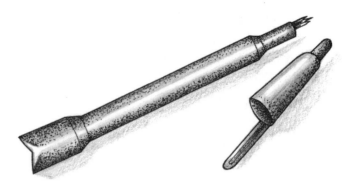

A single tattoo needle.

5. Use the fine-tip felt pen to write the tattoo number on the top of the left ear for guidelines.

6. Place the eraser under the ear to give it a hard backing and to protect your fingers should you poke all the way through the ear.

7. Dip the needle into the ink in the lid or small container.

8. Using the needle at a slight angle, poke a hole in the ear along the guidelines. This places a drop of ink just under the skin.

9. Place the needle back in the ink before each poke and continue until the tattooing is done.

10. Gently clean any excess ink off the ear so you can read the tattoo easily.

11. Place the guinea pig back in its cage and give it a small treat.

12. Check the ear for infection once a day for 2 or 3 days.

Record-keeping

Keep your written records current. The longer you put off your paper work, the bigger the chance that you will make a mistake that could be costly.

Pedigrees

Write the pedigrees for the new pups that have just been weaned. Information on a pedigree covers all the pertinent information about each pup (name, ear number, breed, variety, color, sex, birth date) as well as names, ear numbers, varieties, and colors of parents, grandparents, and great grandparents. Such information can be invaluable and will help potential buyers to spot specific ancestors or colors for which they are breeding.

If guinea pigs in your breeding stock have pedigrees, it is easy to fill out a complete pedigree for each pup. If your breeding stock does not have pedigrees, then you will have to be content with partial pedigrees, for even a partial pedigree is better than nothing.

Keep all your pedigrees in a binder in paper protectors or in a file folder.

Registration

If your guinea pigs have complete pedigrees and do well in shows, you may wish to have them registered. A registered guinea pig has a Certificate of Registration which means that it has passed examination by a Licensed Registrar. A *registrar* is a person who is allowed to register guinea pigs that meet the requirements of the *Standard of Perfection*, with no disqualifications or eliminations. At the time of registration, a registration tag with the registration number is placed in the right ear of the guinea pig.

To register a guinea pig, you must be a member of A.R.B.A. and your guinea pig must be at least 6 months old and weigh over 32 ounces. There is a small fee for registration. Keep Certificates of Registration with your pedigrees.

You can register your guinea pigs at A.R.B.A.-sanctioned shows; you may also be able to get a registrar to come to your home if you have a number of guinea pigs to register.

Make Your Own Pedigrees

You may copy the blank pedigree and accompanying breed pictures on page 136 to use for making your pedigrees. Copy the pedigree and breed pictures, then cut and paste the picture of your breed on the blank pedigree. Now make copies of the completed blank pedigree with the breed picture. Fill these out as you need them. Try not to leave out any information unless there is no way you can get it.

Curran's Fur Fang & Feather Farm

Wanda L. Curran
PO Box 001
Homeville, CA 95965
(009) 555-1234

Sire *CF Shamus*
Ear *CF 36*   Reg.
Color *TSW*
Wt.   G.C.
Winnings:

Breed *Peruvian*
Born *08/04/93*
Sex *SOW*
Name *CG Lilith*
Ear *CF43*   Reg.
Color *TSW*
Wt.   G.C.
Winnings:

Dam *CF Gillian*
Ear *CF30*   Reg.
Color *White/Red*
Wt.   G.C.
Winnings:

Sire *CF Bosco*
Ear *CF9*   Reg.
Color *White/Chocolate*
Wt.   G.C.
Winnings:

Dam *CF Gertie*
Ear *CF20*   Reg.
Color *TSW*
Wt.   G.C.
Winnings:

Sire *Cavy Caper's Showtime*
Ear *PSC25* Reg.
Color *White/Red*
Wt.   G.C.
Winnings:

Dam *CF Lacy*
Ear *CF14*   Reg.
Color *White/Red*
Wt.   G.C.
Winnings:

Sire *Shenanigans Gulliver*
Ear *S16*   Reg.
Color *TSW*
Wt.   G.C.
Winnings:

Dam *Corey's June Bug*
Ear *MAY*   Reg.
Color *White/Black*
Wt.   G.C.
Winnings:

Sire *BEK's Spike*
Ear *PSC45* Reg. A507
Color *Tri Roan*
Wt.   G.C.
Winnings:

Dam *Moon's Melodie*
Ear *PSC7*   Reg.
Color *White/Red*
Wt.   G.C.
Winnings:

Sire *Cavy Caper's Melvin*
Ear   Reg.
Color *White/Cream*
Wt.   G.C.
Winnings:

Dam *Cavy Caper's Mariann*
Ear   Reg.
Color *White/Red*
Wt.   G.C.
Winnings:

Sire *Noah*
Ear *CF4*   Reg. *A506*
Color *TSW*
Wt.   G.C.
Winnings: *"BOSB HRPA
Eureka, CA 03/91*

Dam *Sassie*
Ear *S12*   Reg.
Color *White/Red*
Wt.   G.C.
Winnings:

Date _____

Sold To _____

Address_____

_____

I certify that this pedigree is correct to the best of my knowledge and belief. _____

Full pedigree

Medical Records

Keep medical records for each of your guinea pigs. If you have been treating an animal for an illness, you should keep a written record of the treatment and the guinea pig's progress. Record the medications and/or equipment that you needed to treat this animal. Note the doses and frequency of the medication used.

Cavy Medical Record

Name _____ Ear Number _____ Sex _____

Birthday _____ Breed _____ Variety _____

Sire _____ Dam _____

Date _____ Diagnosis _____
Treatment _____

Observations/Progress _____
_____

Date _____ Diagnosis _____
Treatment _____

Observations/Progress _____
_____

Date _____ Diagnosis _____
Treatment _____

Observations/Progress _____
_____

Date _____ Diagnosis _____
Treatment _____

Observations/Progress _____
_____

Date _____ Diagnosis _____
Treatment _____

Observations/Progress _____
_____

Date _____ Diagnosis _____
Treatment _____

Observations/Progress _____
_____

Date _____ Diagnosis _____
Treatment _____

Observations/Progress _____
_____

Medical record

Breeding Records

Keep breeding records for sows and boars: breeding date, to which boar, when kindled, how many pups delivered, how many pups live/dead. Were there any problems with the sow during pregnancy or birth?

Cavy Breeding Record

Sow _____ Ear Number _____ Birth Date _____
Breed _____ Variety _____
Sire _____ Dam _____

Date Introduced _____
Boar _____ Ear Number _____ Birth Date _____
Breed _____ Variety _____
Date Pregnancy Noted _____ Date Kickers Noted _____
Date Boar Removed _____ Date Delivered _____
Number Live Pups _____ Number Dead Pups _____
Number Raised _____ Pup Varieties/Colors _____

Pregnancy/Delivery Problems _____
_____
_____

Date Introduced _____
Boar _____ Ear Number _____ Birth Date _____
Breed _____ Variety _____
Date Pregnancy Noted _____ Date Kickers Noted _____
Date Boar Removed _____ Date Delivered _____
Number Live Pups _____ Number Dead Pups _____
Number Raised _____ Pup Varieties/Colors _____

Pregnancy/Delivery Problems _____
_____
_____

Date Introduced _____
Boar _____ Ear Number _____ Birth Date _____
Breed _____ Variety _____
Date Pregnancy Noted _____ Date Kickers Noted _____
Date Boar Removed _____ Date Delivered _____
Number Live Pups _____ Number Dead Pups _____
Number Raised _____ Pup Varieties/Colors _____

Pregnancy/Delivery Problems _____
_____
_____

Breeding
record

Financial Records

Keep financial records of feed and supplies that you buy for your caviary. You should also include expenses incurred for going to shows. In addition, keep records of any income from animals that you have sold.

Cavy Financial Record

Expenses

Date	Quantity	Description	Unit Cost	Amount
			Total	

Expense record

Cavy Financial Record

Income/Value

Date	Quantity	Description	Unit Cost	Amount
			Total	

Income record

Show Records

Show records should include what show, who was shown, how it placed, how many in the class, variety, or breed, and the name of the judge.

Cavy Show Record

Name_____ Ear Number_____ Birth Date_____
Breed _____ Variety_____
Sire_____ Dam _____

Date_____ Show_____Location_____
Judge_____
Number in Class/Variety/Breed_____
Place_____ Specials _____
Comments_____
_____

Date_____ Show_____Location_____
Judge_____
Number in Class/Variety/Breed _____
Place_____ Specials_____
Comments _____
_____

Date_____ Show_____Location_____
Judge_____
Number in Class/Variety/Breed_____
Place_____ Specials _____
Comments_____
_____

Date_____ Show_____Location_____
Judge_____
Number in Class/Variety/Breed _____
Place_____ Specials _____
Comments_____
_____

Date_____ Show_____Location_____
Judge_____
Number in Class/Variety/Breed _____
Place_____ Specials _____
Comments_____
_____

Date_____ Show_____Location_____
Judge_____
Number in Class/Variety/Breed_____
Place_____ Specials_____
Comments_____
_____

Activities For Young Guinea Pig Owners

No matter how much you enjoy your guinea pigs, you will find that it really helps to have friends with the same interests and problems. There are times when caring for your guinea pigs may be more of a chore than fun, or you may be frustrated about something happening in your caviary. Being able to talk with friends who may be in the same situation can help a great deal. Sometimes they can come up with solutions to problems that you are having, or you may be able to help them.

Where can you meet other guinea pig raisers?

4-H

4-H is an organization that has cavy projects. You can attend regular project meetings and learn information that is not covered in this particular book. You may be able to participate in a cavy show as a member of the show committee.

Skills

You can learn many new skills in 4-H. These new skills may help you in selling your guinea pigs and dealing with the public.

Other 4-H Activities

There are also many other fun things to do in 4-H. You can exhibit your guinea pigs, do demonstrations, be a member of a cavy quiz bowl team (a team that competes against other teams to answer questions about cavies). You can attend special workshops in areas of interest. You can learn leadership skills as a junior or teen leader, which can be fun and very rewarding.

As a 4-H member, you have opportunities to perform different types of community service. You might take your guinea pigs to nursing homes or schools to teach and/or entertain. You may participate in a health fair and make a presentation about how raising guinea pigs can be an example of an alternative to using drugs.

Fees

There is a small fee to join some 4-H clubs. The fee covers the cost of monthly publications and necessary insurance coverage. Uniforms are usually not required (these are used mainly for fairs), so the cost of participating is lower than many other youth organizations.

Finding Your Local 4-H Office

You will find the address and telephone number of your county 4-H office in the telephone book. It may be listed under 4-H Clubs, under Cooperative Extension, or under the name of your county. Or contact your state 4-H office and ask how to get in touch with your local office.

American Rabbit Breeders Association

The American Rabbit Breeders Association (A.R.B.A.) is a national organization for both adults and youth. There are many activities in which youth may participate.

National Convention

The National A.R.B.A. Convention is the largest cavy show that you and other youth members can attend. There are many contests held at the convention and many other contests in which you can take part, even if you cannot attend the convention.

The management, achievement, and education contests may be entered without attending the convention. You can see how your husbandry and management skills compare with other youth, in the same age group or caviary size, by entering the management and/or achievement contests. You can show off your art and communication skills by entering the education contest with a poster, game, drawing, painting or by using some other skill you may possess.

If you attend the convention, you can take part in the cavy-judging contest or the royalty contest for your age group. You will need to apply, however, for either contest *before* the convention. Complete rules and information for all A.R.B.A. contests are included in the A.R.B.A. Yearbook, which you receive when you become a member. A portion of the royalty contest consists of a written test, a breed identification, and a personal interview. In the interview, you will be asked questions about your project, your interests, your achievements, and your goals. You will receive scores in each area that will be totaled for a final score to decide if you will be that year's A.R.B.A. Cavy King, Queen, Prince, Princess, Duke, Duchess, Lord, or Lady.

Fees

Membership in A.R.B.A. is only $8.00 per year, and you receive the A.R.B.A. Guidebook, the Yearbook with all members listed, and the *Domestic Rabbit* magazine.

Becoming an A.R.B.A. Member

You may become a member of the A.R.B.A. by writing to American Rabbit Breeders Association, Inc., P.O. Box 426, Bloomington, IL 61702.

American Cavy Breeders Association

You may also join The American Cavy Breeders Association (A.C.B.A.), the club that is devoted especially to cavies. To become a member, write to the American Cavy Breeders Association, c/o Mary Guthrie, 22859 Fall Leaf Road, Linwood, KS 66052. The membership fee is $8.00 per year, and you receive the A.C.B.A. Guidebook, Yearbook, and *Journal of the American Cavy Breeders Association* (the A.C.B.A. quarterly magazine).

Other Activities

Your interest in guinea pigs may also help you in school. You may be able to use your guinea pigs to participate in science fairs and to help you write research papers. You may find that by giving an oral report about your guinea pigs, you may introduce other students to this interesting hobby.

_____
(Caviary Name)

Breeder _____
Address _____
Telephone _____

Breed _____
Born ____ Sex _____
Name_____
Ear _____ Reg. _____
Color_____
Wt. _____ G.C. _____
Winnings: _____

Sire _____
Ear_____ Reg. _____
Color_____
Wt. _____ G.C. _____
Winnings: _____

Dam _____
Ear_____ Reg. _____
Color _____
Wt. _____ G.C. _____
Winnings: _____

Sire _____
Ear_____ Reg. _____
Color_____
Wt. _____ G.C. _____
Winnings: _____

Dam _____
Ear_____ Reg. _____
Color_____
Wt. _____ G.C. _____
Winnings: _____

Sire _____
Ear_____ Reg. _____
Color_____
Wt. _____ G.C. _____
Winnings: _____

Dam _____
Ear_____ Reg. _____
Color_____
Wt. _____ G.C. _____
Winnings: _____

Sire _____
Ear_____ Reg._____
Color_____
Wt. _____ G.C. _____
Winnings: _____

Sire _____
Ear_____ Reg._____
Color_____
Wt. _____ G.C. _____
Winnings: _____

Dam _____
Ear _____ Reg._____
Color_____
Wt. _____ G.C. _____
Winnings: _____

Sire _____
Ear_____ Reg _____
Color_____
Wt. _____ G.C._____
Winnings: _____

Dam _____
Ear   Reg.
Color
Wt.   G.C.
Winnings:

Sire _____
Ear_____ Reg._____
Color_____
Wt. _____ G.C. _____
Winnings: _____

Dam _____
Ear_____ Reg. _____
Color _____
Wt. _____ G.C. _____
Winnings: _____

Sire _____
Ear_____ Reg._____
Color _____
Wt. _____ G.C. _____
Winnings: _____

Dam _____
Ear _____ Reg. _____
Color _____
Wt. _____ G.C. _____
Winnings: _____

Date _____

Sold To _____

Address _____

_____

I certify that this pedigree is correct to the best of my knowledge
and belief. _____

You can copy this blank pedigree and use it for your guinea pigs.

Guinea Pig Breeds

Abyssinian

American

Peruvian

Silkie

Teddy

White Crested

Helpful Sources

Mail-Order Rabbitry/ Cavy Suppliers

Most of the following companies will send you a free catalog if you call or write to request one. They are usually fast and reliable. Local breeders may be able to give you more names of companies that are closer to your location. There may even be a cavy supplier in your city. Check the yellow pages in your local telephone book.

Bass Equipment Company
P.O. Box 352
Monett, MO 65708
417-235-7557
800-798-0150
Fax 417-235-4312

Bass Western Warehouse
11264 Eastside Rd.
Healdsburg, CA 95448
707-433-6177
800-369-7518

Da-Mars Equipment Co.
14468 Industrial Parkway
So. Beloit, IL 61080
815-624-2672
815-624-2670
Fax 815-624-2883

Fry Equipment Company
6315 S. Hydraulic
Wichita, KS 67216
316-524-5413

Klubertanz Equipment Company, Inc.
1165 R Hwy. 73
Edgerton, WI 53534
608-884-9481
800-237-3899

K W Cages Manufacturing
1250 Pioneer Way
El Cajon, CA 92020
800-447-CAGE
in California 619-447-6000
Fax 619-447-8527

Safeguard
P.O.Box 8
New Holland, PA 17557
800-433-1819

Valentine Equipment Co.
7510 S. Madison Street
P.O.Box 487
Hinsdale, IL 60522
708-323-7070
Fax 312-650-9099

Wolf Cage & Supply
0885 N. 650 W
Kimmell, IN 46760
219-635-2356

Recommended Reading

The Wonderful World of Cavies 6th Edition 1993 by Golden State Cavy Breeders Association, 3727 N. Ranchford Ct., Concord, CA 94520.

The Biology and Medicine of Rabbits and Rodents by John E. Harkness, Joseph E. Wagner. Lea & Febiger, Philadelphia, PA 1989.

A Guide to Diagnosis, Treatment, and Husbandry of Pet Rabbits and Rodents by Robert J. Russell, D.V.M.; David K. Johnson, D.V.M.; Jim A. Stunkard, D.V.M. Veterinary Medicine Publishing Co., Edwardsville, KS 1989.

A Rainbow of Guinea Pigs; Cavies, A Guide Book of Cavy Lore Book I & II 1990-91. Edited by Jim Mc Corpin, 9215 Sandstone, Houston, TX 77036. (There is a third book in the making.)

The Standard of Perfection, A.R.B.A., P.O. Box 426, Bloomington, IL 61702.

Associations

American Cavy Breeders Association (A.C.B.A.)
c/o Mary Guthrie
22859 Fall Leaf Road
Linwood, KS 66052

American Rabbit Breeders Association (A.R.B.A.)
P.O. Box 426
Bloomington, IL 61702
Telephone: 309-827-6623

Veterinarian's Treatments

A Note to Veterinarians Treating Guinea Pigs

The following are accepted practices for treatment of certain guinea pig illnesses that cannot be treated at home or in cases where the recommended home treatment has not been effective. (Those treatments and remedies are found in Chapter 4 of this book.)

Pneumonia

1. Trimethoprim Sulfa (Septra, TMP-SMZ, Tribrissen) 240 milligrams/5 milliliters (240 milligrams/teaspoon), .5 milliliters per pound of weight, twice daily.

2. Baytril, injectable 22.7 milligrams/milliliter, 1 to 2 milligrams per pound, twice daily; or tablets, 5 milligrams, $\frac{1}{4}$ tablet for animals less than 1 pound, $\frac{1}{2}$ tablet for those over 1 pound, twice daily. (Do not attempt to put injectable Baytril into drinking water. It doesn't work.)

Diarrhea

1. Sulfamethazine 12.5% in drinking water, 1 teaspoon in 8 ounces of water until diarrhea is gone for 3 days. Or terramycin powder in drinking water, 1 tablespoon in 1 gallon of water until diarrhea is gone for 3 days. Or Albon 240 milligrams per teaspoon, 1 ml ($\frac{1}{4}$ teaspoon) for 7 days.

2. Give live culture yogurt or acidophilus water ($\frac{1}{4}$ to $\frac{1}{2}$ capsule in 8 ounces of water) by mouth 4 to 6 times daily during treatment with antibiotic, and for 3 days after antibiotic is discontinued.

Heatstroke

Administer subcutaneous fluids (fluids given under the skin), lactated Ringer's and 0.45% saline with 2.5% dextrose — 10 to 15 cc in neck 1 to 2 times a day as needed.

Ringworm (Fungus)

Note that griseofulvin should be considered an absolute last resort for treatment of fungus.

Vaginal Infection

1. Albon 240 milligrams per teaspoon, 1 milliliter (¼ teaspoon) twice daily for 7 days or until signs/symptoms are gone.

2. Acidophilus water (¼ to ½ to ½ acidophilus capsule in 8 ounces of water) between doses of medication.

Torticollis

1. Albon 240 milligrams per teaspoon, to 1 milliliter (¼ teaspoon) twice daily for 7 days. Or baytril, ½ 5 milligram tablet (¼ tablet for animals under 1 pound) every 12 hours for 7 to 10 days (use a small piller if necessary).

2. Acidophilus water (¼ to ½ acidophilus capsule in 8 ounces of water) between doses of medication.

3. Force fluids and feed if guinea pig is not drinking and eating. (See treatment for colds, page 138.)

Glossary

afterbirth (n). The placenta and membranes that deliver nutrients from the sow's blood to the unborn pups' blood and remove waste from the unborn pups' blood. Each pup's placenta and membranes are expelled from the sow after the pup is born.

agouti (n., adj.). A variety of cavy having a dark base color with evenly distributed ticking over the body except for the bellyband. Bellyband color is to match the tip color of the hair and there is no ticking.

boar (n.). A male cavy.

breed (n.). A class of cavy that reproduces its own distinct characteristics: hair growth pattern, type, size, etc.

brindle (n., adj.). The coat color that results from the intermingling of red hair and black hair; every other hair to be red or black. The coat must have intermingling of red and black of at least 60% to be a showable brindle.

broken coat (n.). Molting or shedding so as to have undercoat showing.

Caesarean section (n.). A surgical procedure on a sow to deliver unborn pups.

caviary (n.). The place where guinea pigs are raised.

cavy (n.). A mammal, commonly called a guinea pig, having no tail, a single pair of mammae, four toes on the front feet, and three toes on the hind feet.

class (n.). A show division determined by age and/or weight and sex.

conceive (v.). Become pregnant.

congenital (adj.). From the time of birth.

crest (n.). The rosette on the forehead of the White Crested.

crossbreed (n.). A guinea pig having parents of different breeds.

Dalmation (n., adj.). A variety of guinea pig, in the marked group, having spots of any self color on a white background.

depth of color (n.). How far down the hair shaft a color extends from the tip toward the skin.

dermatitus (n.). Inflammation of the skin.

dilate (v.). To open or separate, as when the pelvic bones of a sow separate to allow the birth of pups.

disqualification (n.). A permanent defect on a guinea pig which makes the guinea pig unshowable, such as a missing tooth.

double rosette (n.). A rosette having two centers instead of one center.

Dutch (n., adj.). A variety of guinea pig, in the marked group, having a white collar, chest, forelegs, blaze, and foot stops. The rest of the guinea pig may be any self or agouti color.

elimination (n.). A temporary defect that makes a guinea pig unshowable until cured.

estrus (n.). The recurrent period when a sow is receptive to a boar and can become pregnant if mating occurs.

faking (v.). Changing the appearance of an animal to deceive judges or buyers.

fault (n.). An imperfection in the appearance of a cavy which does not eliminate or disqualify the animal.

foot stops (n.). White markings on the hind feet of the Dutch variety of guinea pig. The markings start at the toes and cover the length of {1/3} of the feet.

frontal (n.). The hair that falls over the face of a Peruvian guinea pig.

gestation (n.). The period of time starting when a sow becomes pregnant and ending when the pups are born.

group (n.). A subdivision in a breed based on hair shaft color and color pattern: self, solid, agouti, marked

heat (n.). The recurrent period when a sow is receptive to a boar and can become pregnant if mating occurs.

herbivorous (adj.). Having a diet restricted only to plants.

hernia (n.). A protrusion of an organ or tissue through an abnormal opening in the muscles causing a soft lump that can be seen and felt.

inbreeding (v.). Breeding guinea pigs that are very closely related (father to daughter, mother to son, brother to sister).

infertility (n.). Inability to conceive or to induce conception.

intermediate (n., adj.). A cavy 4 to 6 months of age, or over 22 ounces and up to and including 32 ounces.

junior (n., adj.). A cavy under 4 months of age, minimum weight of 12 ounces, maximum weight of 22 ounces.

kindle (v.). To give birth.

labor (n.). The process of giving birth.

leg (n.). Certificate awarded to cavy by a licensed cavy judge at an officially sanctioned A.R.B.A. show where there are three breeders and five cavies in the class, variety, or breed. A cavy needs three legs to be eligible for a Grand Champion Certificate.

line breeding (v.). Breeding guinea pigs with a common ancestor (having same father but different mothers, having same grandfather or grand-mother).

litter (n.). The young born to a sow from a single breeding.

luster (n.). The amount of shine a normal coat has.

malocclusion (n.). Teeth that do not meet properly.

mammae (n.). Plural of mammary. Glands in a sow that produce milk to nourish young pups.

marked (n., adj.). Having patches of color placed in very specific spots, or having only certain colors for markings.

mastitis (n.). An inflammation of the mammary.

metabolizing (v.). The way a body of a living thing uses food to produce energy for life.

milk sop (n.). Bread crumbs soaked in cow's milk used to supplement a sow's milk.

outbreeding (v.). The practice of breeding guinea pigs that are totally unrelated.

patch (n.). An area of color surrounded by one or more different colors.

pea eye (n.). A hereditary condition in which a lump forms in the lower eyelid.

pedigree (n.). A document provided by the seller attesting to the purebred lines of a cavy for at least three previous generations.

placenta (n.). The tissue that allows delivery of nutrients from the sow's blood to the unborn pups' blood and removal of waste from the unborn pups' blood to the sow's blood.

polydactyl (adj.). Having an extra toe or toes.

pruritus (n.). Itching.

purebred (adj.). A guinea pig having parents of the same breed and all its ancestors are of the same breed.

quarantine (v.). To isolate or separate guinea pigs that are ill or new from healthy guinea pigs to prevent the spread of illness.

ramrod (n.). The person, at a judging table during a show, who takes guinea pigs from exhibitors, makes sure all animals in a class are on the judging table, then places the guinea pigs in judging coops. After judging is completed, the ramrod returns guinea pigs to the exhibitors.

registered (adj.). A guinea pig having a Certificate of Registration and a registration tag indicating that the guinea pig has a three-generation pedigree, and has passed an examination by a licensed registrar.

roan (n., adj.). The coat color produced by the intermingling of white hair with any other color hair; every other hair to be white or any accepted color.

rodent (n.). Mammal with large incisors adapted for gnawing (mouse, rat, hamster, gerbil, guinea pig).

rosette (n.). The radiated pattern of hair growth from a center point seen on Abyssinian, Abyssinian Satin, and White Crested guinea pigs.

self or self-colored (n., adj.). Having the same color of hair all over the body; the hair shaft is only one color from tip to base.

senior (n., adj.). A cavy 6 months of age and over, or weighing over 32 ounces.

shedding (v.). Losing hair so that new hair can grow in.

sheen (n.). The amount of shine a satin coat has.

solid or solid-colored (n., adj.). Having the same uniform color over the whole body; the hair shaft may have different base and tip colors, there may be ticking, and there may be intermingling of two colors of hair. There are no markings.

sow (n.). A female guinea pig.

ticking (n.). Longer guard hair distributed throughout the hair that is the same color as the undercolor.

tipping (n.). The color at the end of the hair shaft on an Agouti, which is a different color from the undercolor.

type (n.). The conformation of a guinea pig (shape, size); the general physical appearance of a guinea pig.

undercolor (n.). The color at the base of the hair shaft next to the skin.

unthrifty (adj.). Having an unhealthy appearance without exhibiting any signs or symptoms of illness.

variety (n.). A subdivision in a breed determined by hair and/or eye color or color pattern.

wean (v.). When a sow gradually stops nursing her young so the young only eat solid food and need no more nourishment from her.

INDEX

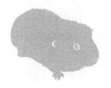